THE
DECADENT
CONSCIOUSNESS

A
HIDDEN ARCHIVE OF LATE
VICTORIAN LITERATURE

FORTY-TWO RARE AND IMPORTANT TITLES
PUBLISHED IN THIRTY-SIX VOLUMES

EDITED BY

IAN FLETCHER &
JOHN STOKES

GARLAND PUBLISHING

FLOWERS OF PASSION

PAGAN POEMS

George Moore

Garland Publishing, Inc., New York & London

1978

Bibliographical note:

These facsimiles have been made from copies
in the Beinecke Library of Yale University
Flowers of Passion (Ip.M783.878F);
and the Bodleian Library of Oxford University
Pagan Poems (280.e.4365).

The volumes in this series have been printed on
acid-free, 250-year-life paper.

Library of Congress Cataloging in Publication Data

Moore, George, 1852-1933.
  Flowers of passion.

  (The Decadent consciousness ; no. 29)
  Reprint of the 1878 ed. of Flowers of passion,
published by Provost, London, and of the 1881 ed. of
the Pagan poems, published by Newman, London.
  I. Moore, George, 1852-1933. Pagan poems. 1978.
II. Title. III. Series.
PR5042.F64 1978   821'.8   76-20138
ISBN 0-8240-2778-7

Printed in the United States of America

FLOWERS OF PASSION.

BY

GEORGE MOORE.

LONDON:

PROVOST & CO., 36, HENRIETTA STREET,
COVENT GARDEN.

1878.

ERRATA.

Page 13, line 18, for *did* read *do*.

„ 18, delete lines 9 and 10.

„ 32, line 1, for *streams* read *strains*.

„ 38, „ 2, „ *charmed* „ *chained*.

CONTENTS.

DEDICATION.

TO L——.

Lean meward, O beloved! let me crown
Thy brows with chaplet.   Votive wreath I twine
Of symbol flowers, and therein weave for sign,
From graft of passion, roses that have grown
Bitter as frothing of blood; yet cast not down
As worthless weeds, but set upon Love's shrine
In vase full filled with memories of mine,
These bloomless blossoms of a time long flown.

Frail fledglings of heart-hidden memories,
Pale passion flowers I bring to thee, my sweet,
As Mary brought her offerings of white doves;
No greater gifts have I to give than these
Of seeds we sowed.   I lay them at thy feet;
For they are thine, and being thine are Love's.

B

FLOWERS OF PASSION.

————◦◦◦————

ODE TO A DEAD BODY.

Is it a garden of eternal sleep
    Where dreams laugh not or weep?
A place of quiet below the tides of life
    Afar from toil or strife?
A deep calm sea our souls may yearn unto
    Where memory never flew?
A darkling void cloaked in a clinging night
    Unstirred by any light?
The tomb is veiled—these are its mysteries,
    That no man ever sees.

O! queen of love discrowned and stripped to-day
    Of all thy gold array
Save the pale gold of thy enwoven hair
    Which drapes thy body bare.
Thou wast in life a creature of the hour,
    No graver than a flower,
A gilded fly who played in the high noon
    Of pleasure's waning moon,
Until at last thou fellest, a withered leaf
    Worth gathering in no sheaf
Of memory, to be upstored and kept
    By none who watched and wept.

Ay verily, thou art a piteous thing,
    So awful is death's sting.
Poor shameful lips! that never knew a kiss
    Of innocence, I wis.

Poor breasts! whose nipples sins alone have fed.
    Poor desecrated head!
Poor lily hands! steeped in the mire of shame,
    Poor heart! whose love ran lame.
Thou hast no lover now, Why have they gone
    And left thee here alone?
Is there not one of all the hundreds who
    Once kissed thee thro' and thro'
In the deep silence of the summer night
    In rapture and delight,
Whose memory a little gold might crave
    And give to thee a grave,
Afar from city's roar, amid tall trees
    In nearing of the seas,
Whose sighing voices whispered in thine ear
    In childhood's happy year,
When thou wast dreaming dreams in the high grass,
    Watching for ships to pass

And fade beneath the long horizon line,
    Taking each for a sign ?

The legends say that 'twas in woman first
    Love's lips grew dry with thirst,
And held to man the poisoned apple Lust,
    Whose core is burning dust
That fills the well-springs of the heart, and dries
    Their sources to arise
No more, and slake the dry Sahara plain
    Of passion and pale pain.
Or do the legends lie, and was it man
    Whose fleshly wings did fan
Those scorching winds whose fiery flame-like breath
    Pursue the soul to death ?
It matters nought, the imminent end is one
    To harlot and to nun,

Virtue and vice conceived in one womb
    Sleep in the self-same tomb.
The head of Lust was coinèd from thy face,
    And bought in market place
Plain passion, and strange sins without a name
    E'en in the lists of shame ;
And thou wast hated, trodden underfoot
    With gibe and laugh and hoot,
And loved and kissed with wild delirious kiss,
    Till Death took thee in his
Breast, laying thee asleep afar from love
    Or any scorn thereof,
Equal to all.   For dust is e'er the same
    And free from taint of shame.

A wondrous race is thine.   Since time began,
    Since love to lust first ran,

And plighted faith was broken and cast down
    As an unkingdomed crown,
And Vice took seat upon the world's high throne
    To reign and rule alone,
And Virtue as his queen was placed beside
    To serve him for a bride,
Hast thou been knelt to and with tears adored,
    And bought with gold and sword.
The grave takes thee, another of thy race
    Soon fills the vacant place,
As rose replaces rose upon the tree
    As sweet each to the bee.
So to the furthest end of history
    The self-same thing shall be,
For lust is love, and love is king o'er kings
    And master of earthly things.

I gaze upon thy face now changed in death
    In fear and awe-held breath,
And ponder if this clay-built tenement
    Be of divine intent;
If for it God has not conceived a soul
    And made a perfect whole
To live transfigured through all change and time
    Immutable, sublime;
Or if 'tis nothing but an instant part
    Of this world's mighty heart,
Wandering thro' space in every shape and form,
    Like changing cloud in storm;
Either may be! two roads to left and right,
    Unknown, both lost in night.

GINEVRA.

SCENE—*A bridge in the city of Verona.*
TIME—*Nearly midnight.*

ANTONIO. If every man had on his brow
  engraved
The sorrow he had known, what mockery
Would pity be! Life's pleasures are but few,
Life's griefs are many, and their end the same.
Yet sometimes in the silent solitude
Sorrow doth seem most like a comforter;
Her very pain is sweet, her very tears
Like oil assuage and calm life's weary waves.
How wonderfully sweet the midnight hour!
How silent and mysteriously still
A city seems by night! Now all is hushed
Beneath the spell of sleep. The heavens lie

Buried in deep repose.   The river flows
Serenely on in silent stateliness;
With all its sad and secret histories
Hidden within a time-unwrinkled breast:
It passes like a dream whose skirt we strive
To seize when waking's nigh eluding us.
How like it is to life!   It comes and goes,
Changing, yet e'er the same.   The domes and
      temples
Lie quivering in its breathless atmosphere,
And are erased by every passing cloud
And every wandering air, like dreams by dreams.
'Tis strange that all must die.   If some bright
      spirit,
Pausing on its aërial way, would tell
To listening ears why rainbows gleam not ever;
Why wind and cloud and fairest flowers must die;
Why all things come and go mysteriously.

Then we should know; the highway would be lit
With light that darkens sun and moon and star,
And we might drink of joy and call life pleasure.
The earth would give no longer thorns to tread,
And sorrow no more bitter tears to weep.
Man, Lord of things, encrowned in wisdom of
    years,
Would sit supreme, God over gods dethroned.

               (*Enter* ORISINO.)

  ORISINO. Heigh ho! Antonio, as usual,
Dreaming some faint sick dream.

  ANTONIO.   What, is it thou?

  ORISINO. Yes, it is I who wake thee from thy
    dreams;
And yet, methinks, withal thou art most carnal,
And lovest well the pleasures of the flesh.
Yea, I will warrant that a lady is
The cause of all this moonlight meditation.

ANTONIO. It may be that thou hast divined it
    rightly.

ORISINO. Well! love is fair and very beautiful.
What sweeter than a tender lily girl,
Who clings to you in devout simplicity,
Like ivy to the oak!

ANTONIO.   It may be so;
But I aver your girls do weary me.
I long for that more spiritual essence
Of soul-predestined love, that, like a star,
Flames burning bright and unconsumably,
Shedding a light and radiance through the deep
And middle night of soul despondency.
And though a distance limitless doth now
Divide me from my soul conceived soul,
Yet I, without sign-manual of love,
Or God, or any human precedent,
Did blindly and unreasoningly adore.

ORISINO. Thy brain is sick with dream and
fantasy.

Hast thou, then, met this shadow of thy soul?

ANTONIO. If I were e'er to speak my secret
mind,

In bitter loathing thou would'st turn from me.

ORISINO. Thou knowest well I never judged
thee harshly;

Since we were boys 'twas I that did excuse thee

When others blamed. Nay! speak, Antonio.

ANTONIO. I tell thee, if I speak, that thou wilt
hate,

Ay, even full as much as thou dost love.

ORISINO. It grieves me sore to hear thee speak
so.

ANTONIO.   Yes,

'Tis as I say; but speak of other things.

ORISINO. Nay, nay, Antonio; 'tis twenty years

Since, on my or on thy dear mother's knee,
(I know not which, for they were loving friends,
As we have been, and were inseparable)
We first did enter into friendship's bonds.

    ANTONIO. I know thou lovest me, thou art my
        friend;
But there are things that some see black as night,
Yet others think as bright and pure as day.
I tremble at my love. The human heart,
Like brooks and wells, has many flowers that
    bloom
Beneath the lucid wave. These flowers ever
Turn their eyes towards the sun, and seek to pierce
The green gloom of the silent atmosphere;
They struggle hard, and when at length their roots
Give way, released they rise to the topmost wave,
And gaze upon the long-imagined sun;
But, like a tame bird in an unknown land,

They find no kinship, only enmity.
The killing insect and the gnawing worm
Soon seize the fragrant blossom, and deflower
Its loveliness.

ORISINO.   If love's attainment be
So cast, why seek predestined bitterness?

ANTONIO. Because 'tis better far to see the sun
And die, than live purblind eternally.

ORISINO. Trust me, Antonio; my counsel will
Help thee, perhaps.

ANTONIO.   Ask me no more, but list.
Long I lay in the shadow of my thought,
Where all was shrouded 'neath the inky veil
Of storm-closed clouds of doubt and misery;
My soul raged like a midnight sea, that writhes
A wounded thing beneath the lashing scourge
Of wind and rain. The storm lulled suddenly,
And a green patch of sky between the clouds

Shone like a burning emerald; green glancing
Shadows played o'er the sea's marmoreal breast,
And, midway 'tween the sea-line and the sky,
A plenilune of love hung motionless;
And myriad stars of joy and hope shone bright
Within the deep unfathomably. It was
My own fair sister, who stood signal-wise,
Lighting the beaconed wintry wilderness
That I called life. The first snow-drop that peeps
From earthly nest, and gazes tremblingly
Upon the bare, bleak world, is not more dear
To mother Spring than this sweet child to me;
But custom's bitter mouth had cursed the love
That might 'tween brother and a sister grow.

    ORISINO (*aside*). Have I gone mad, or do I hear
      aright?
My brain reels round; I feel a dizzy sickness
Seize hold on me; a something glues my lips

And clings, and eats into my very bones.
I am like one in loathsome charnel pit
Where things are veiled in pestilential haze.
Pah! What a nauseous hell-born infamy!
My hand would stab him in the very mouth,
Would pluck forth by the roots that fetid weed,
His tongue, and cast it to the dogs.   But no,
The dogs would vomit sick with loathing hate.
No mouth could hold a thing so poisonous
Except his own.
And this is whom I loved.   What scorpion
Lay in my breast!   But I will listen yet
Tho' his words sting me unto bitter death.

   ANTONIO. Our father first encouraged our sweet
      love,
But when at length the whole truth dawned on him,
He tried by threats and prayers to wean us from
What he did blindly term unholy passion;

But finding then, too late, it was most useless
To separate two hearts that love had joined,
He prisoned her within a convent wall.

  ORISINO. Most merciful God! my cup of bitter-
    ness
Indeed is full, aye filled to overflowing:
To know the girl that I thought pure and chaste,
So black, so false, and full of infamy,
The girl I loved with a great unuttered love.

                    (*Searches for dagger.*)

Not now, the guard comes by.   It must be done
Most silently and secretly.

          (*Soldiers pass singing.*)
    Fill high the stoup of wine; fill high,
       And drink to our sweethearts dear;
    We laugh and sing but never sigh,
       Unless in a lady's ear.

                    C 2

(Chorus.)

A soldier's life, a soldier's life,
　A soldier's life for me ;
In every town we have a wife,
　In every city three.

Antonio.　What noise those roistering fellows make;
　　　　　　　　　　　　　　　　[one's speech
Is drowned in utterance.

　　　　　　　　This very night
I meet her in the convent cemetery.
Love lends her wings to pass the gate and wall,
And she will fly with me to some far land,
Where none will ever know the double love
That binds us two.

　　　　　　　What thinkest thou ?　My plan,
Does it not seem to thee most feasible ?
The strangeness of my love bewilders thee;
The prejudice of years and teaching blinds.

Sweetness can ne'er be wrong. Nay, thou wilt
    help
And aid me. Why those passion-pale bent brows?
  ORISINO. I prithee, pardon. Th' wildness of
    thy words,
The darkness of the night, a hundred things,
Unnerve my thoughts.

            (*Aside.*) I'll let him meet her there,
And then, before her very eyes, this steel
Shall kiss his foul black heart, and send his soul
To writhe in darkness of tempestuous fire.
Then, long sweet years of undiminished love,
And prayers and hopes will I lay round her feet ;
And, if from this most baneful lust I wean
Her once bright pure ethereal soul, my life
Will have attained its furthest end.

SCENE II.

An old ruinous cemetery, ivy-grown walls, dilapidated, tombs and gravestones.

(*Enter* ANTONIO *and* ORISINO.)

ANTONIO. No sound disturbs the night. Wild clouds like hounds

A weary moon do chase thro' starless fields

Of wintry sky. The wandering wind doth sigh,

As might a spectre lady sorrowing

Around the nuptial bed of her beloved.

The yews and cypresses, the waving grass,

Seem instinct with the grave. How painfully

Those whitening willows swing their mystic branches

On every passing air. Do they not seem

To whisper to the mist-wrought phantom forms

That rise from out the wormy earth, and float

Folding themselves into a hundred shapes,

Divided by the wind.   The tomb-cast shadows

Steal weirdly to and fro winding across

The cemetery.   How pallid is the light

Of the cold smitten moon!   Here all is death,

And images of death.   This silent earth

Holds men and maids who loved ; holds sin and
  crime,

Strange hates and bitter wretchedness.   O Earth !

Thou mother of us all, I kiss thy face,

I brush my cheek amid thy grass and leaves.

Thou art the final end ; thou askest nought,

Thy mute lips question not ; thou givest peace

To harlot and to nun, to atheist

And priest, alike, a sweet eternal peace.

  ORISINO. Methinks the scene is not the cheer-
    fullest.

You do but dream.   The place oppresses me,

This gravestone 's opportune, let us sit here.
Some minutes yet must pass before the hour
Doth strike, that day from night divides.   But
    hark !
What is that awful penetrating sound ?
It fills the mind with fearful trembling.

(Chorus of Nuns.)

From out of the deep sea of time, we arise,
Whose depths are unstirred by the pulse of the
    years,
Whose waters are waveless, unbittered with tears ;
Where all is a sleep without ears, without eyes ;
We arise, we awake, on the stroke of the hour
When virginal love blooms into an infinite flower.

From out of the deep sea of time, we awake,
Where sleep has no current, nor tide to upcast

The tall foundered wrecks of the pale dead past;
Where the stars of the future ne'er tremble and
    break;
We arise, we awake, for the dawning is near,
And is whitening the surge of the hours that pour
    out the year.

(*Voices from above.*)
Our passions sustain us, and move
To the motion of instinct desire;
With the rhythmical anguish of love,
And the heaving of tremulous fire.

(*Voices from below.*)
The thirst unassuaged yet unsloken
Will be drowned in the fiercest delight;
And love will be rent and be broken,
And kissed out of feeling or sight.

(*A Voice.*)

Our virtue resisted
The passion, that twisted
The sense in its coils, till our senses were withered
 and sere.

(*Another Voice.*)

Now all that love's passion
Can mould, or can fashion,
We will know, we will taste, this night of the
 hundredth year.

(*Voices from above.*)

We nestle, like nestling of doves,
We hover on shadowing wings,
O'er the eyes and the lips of loves
Dreaming unreachable things.

(*A Voice.*)

No love will be rootless,

No joy will be fruitless,

All things will be sweet, and passion the thing
the most dear.

(*Voices from below.*)

The shuddering of eyelids and lips ;

The trembling of senses that die;

The spirit too weary, that trips

And falls like the breath in a sigh.

(*Chorus of Nuns and Virgins.*)

Laid low by the gods in the deep,

In the deep below vision or dream,

Where the worm her vigil doth keep

Together with the soul supreme ;

On the threshold of Adenn, we seem

To gaze down a vista of light,
To float on a magical stream,
In the sight
Of delight
That is seen like a gleam through the night.
We have wandered
A hundred
Dim weary years on the bound,
On the limits of heaven and earth, awaiting the
[trumpet to sound.

Unmingled with passion for leaven,
Our love grew as bitter as dust;
And we gazed on unreachable heaven,
Leaving our bodies to rust.
We arise from the earth, for we must,
With lips all alive with desire,
With sense o'erladen with lust;

Like the fire

Of a pyre,

Like the tones of a vibrating lyre,

Like the moon,

In a swoon

Of love on the bosom of night,

Our senses are panting, are trembling, and faint-
ing, i' a dream of delight.

(*A Voice.*)

Oh, take ye and eat,

Our love is most sweet;

Our lips are as honey, our bosom the milk of desire.

(*Voices from above.*)

Come, kiss ere the dawn be risen,

Our kisses are strange and unknown;

Come, sleep in our bosom's fair prison,

Till pleasure be bloomless and blown.

(Another Voice.)
Our limbs are as white
As snow in the night ;
Our breath is as balm when the soul sinks down
to expire.

(Voices from below.)
We mete out a measure of passion,
A measure of mixed gall and wine ;
And love we re-model and fashion,
Till love doth sink down supine.

(Semi-chorus of Nuns and Maidens.)
To love's translucid waters
We immaculate daughters
Pass on, arrayed and garlanded as brides ;
Athirst with love's sweet want,
Around the sacred font

We kneel, and pray for love and what besides,
      With bent reverted heads
And faces veiled, awaiting Love's communion
                    [breads.

ANTONIO. I hear sweet singing in the upper air,
That fills mine ear with strange, sweet harmony;
My soul doth beat her wings in vain endeavour
To break the prison bars, that sepulchre
The spirit in this tenement of clay,
And wander forth in the untainted air.

   ORISINO. My heart is dead. It is not mortal
      music.

   ANTONIO. List well. Their voices are with
      lightning crowned;
They roll like thunder on the midnight wind,
Ebbing and flowing like advancing tides;
And, as each white crest rears, and falling swells
In wild majestic consonance, pausing

A moment, that the two united streams
May fall in justly-balanced unison,
Note how each separate wave of sound doth rise
In one undeviating mystic measure.

   ORISINO. A moment hence those clouds of
     phantom forms
Did whiten in their flight the vault of heaven.
They seem to pass away, and I to think
That all was but a dream's imaginings.
But, lo! they are now nearer than before.
My God! they seem to sweep, to touch the earth.
I hear a rush of wings.　A sense of dread
That lifts the hair on end, an icy glare
And the damp smell of clay cling round my lips.
Does not one glide from their receding ranks?
Methinks I see a woman standing there.
Woman or ghost, I know not which, or what,
This night has been so terrible.

ANTONIO. O where?

ORISINO. Beneath the moon.

ANTONIO. That white-robed maiden there,
So wild, so strangely, beautifully bright:
Her faultless form is seen so varyingly,
Seeming beneath her transitory robe
Like restless gossamer; her pale white hands
Are moveless as dead things; her eyelashes
Are worn away with tears. From her faint lips
Colour and smile seem to have fled for ever.
Toward us she doth glide. Her golden hair
Cloud-like floats down the wind of her own
    speed.
'Tis she whom I have waited for so long,
It is my sister.

    (*Rushes forward into her arms, but starts back
        as soon as he touches her.*)

D

ORISINO. The time is now arrived, his days are
 counted.

  (*He draws his dagger.* GINEVRA *waves her
  hand, the dagger falls.*)

The terror of the night unnerves my will,
I shake as if with ague, my hand, palsied,
Falls like a dead thing useless : but the sight
Of their incestuous love sends new blood back,
Filling the wells and springs of my weak heart.

  (*He draws his sword, she waves her hand, and
  the sword breaks.*)

What devilish spells are these ?   But though
 he be
Leagued by a million bonds to the Evil One,
He shall not now escape my just vengeance.
Thy spells are vain, my hands will strangle thee.

   (*Tries to advance, but retreats instead.*)

Scene III.

Room in the house of Antonio.
Antonio and Ginevra *sitting on a couch.*

Antonio. My love doth take one like the sea;
    it swells   [dreams
With wash of thickening waters, when sweet
Make its heart leap with such a might of joy
As hurls its waves together, and then again
When they have fled into their furthest caves,
And left its bosom glassy as a mirror,
I gaze therein upon the tearful face
Of my despair.   Thou art too lovely, sweet.
I can but close my eyes, and dream a dream
Of many strange and feverish agonies.
O love! thou knowest not how weak I am;
How overlaid my soul is with desire
That longs yet loathes. This hour has come at last.

                        D 2

How I have sighed for it! how it has been
Bound up within my life as the end of all !
The supreme, gracious end that life might pour
Into her vase, till all was overflowed
With very sweetness.   Turn meward thy lips,
That chalice ruby-wrought.   Let loose, let slide
Thy girdle's clasp, I fain would kiss thy bosom,
Those snow-white roses, blooming into red.
There let me lay my head, and dream away
What we call life; and firewise let love burn
And smoulder into ash.   Nay, nay, my sweet,
Let me weave thy soft hair around thy hands,
Tying the other braid across my throat,
I would so sweet a rope might strangle me.

                              (*He kisses her.*)

Thy cheeks are cold, more chilly than the snow ;
Thine eyes are glassy like a midnight sea,
And thy lips hold a pale and moony smile,

As in a dream's strange wild imaginings.
I clasp thy fair sweet body in my arms,
But it doth freeze my breast that burns with love.
Oh! why that wild and wonder-stricken air?
Knowest not me! thine own Antonio.
Lie closer on me, breathe the fire
Of love in thee.

           Is this the wandering
Of insane brain?   Ginevra! art thou dead
Before the fulfilment of my love? Ginevra!
Speak one low whispered word to me, and say
That thou dost live.

Scene IV.

Outside the door of ANTONIO'S *chamber.*

ORISINO (*listening*). I hear their mingling voices,
Like cooing doves in newly-budding trees:

I hear kiss laid on kiss, sigh breathed on sigh.
What super-human power has charmed my will?
I will, but cannot act.   Most merciful God
Thou hast revealed to me the agony
And bloody sweat of dire Gethsemane,
The scourging of the pillar, the crown of thorns,
The cracking, splitting nerves, and racked joints
Of three hours' crucifixion.   Thine anguish
I here do feel, O God! bound, crucified.

Scene inside.

(ANTONIO *kisses* GINEVRA, *but starts back as
if stung.*)

ANTONIO.   The same cold corpse-like chill, the
   livid hue,
The wan and sunken outline as before.
Ginevra! art thou dead?   Ginevra, speak!

Speak, or my brain goes mad with agony.

   GINEVRA. When from her antenatal dreams the
     moth
Doth prune her trembling wing, and soars away
Amid the sunny skies and sweet spring flowers,
She leaves behind an empty chrysalis:
Like her, we mortals cast a shell called life,
When the soul spreads her pinions heavenward
To flowerful fields of immortality.
The gates of love are the outer gates of heaven,
Each thought a step toward the spirit divine,
Each deed a link of one stupendous chain
Stretching from depth to height. Good bye, O!
     brother,
Soon we beyond the portals of the tomb
Shall meet for ever.

                (GINEVRA *vanishes*.)

   ANTONIO.   I must be mad, or dream;

I stretch my arms and clasp but yielding air.
The lips and hands I kissed, the eyes that gazed
In love and fear, the faultless, peerless form
That these arms held in amorous embrace,
Are dissolved into unsubstantial air.
I must be mad or dream.   Here is the place
Her leaned back head did bow the pillows in
When my lips closed upon the fragrant flower
Of her sweet breast, kissed till the pained blood
    quivered.
Art thou gone? speak; my brain reels dizzy, speak!
My breath doth take me by the throat, a chill
Lays icy hand upon me, the pavement sinks
Beneath my feet, my eyes are blind with blood.
I strive to catch my thoughts that swoop meward
Like hawks that stoop, but to the lure to strike,
And tear at it with ravening beak and talon,
And then uncaptured slide back in high air.

ORISINO (*rushing in*). Thy spells are broken now,
    my will asserts
Again its sovereignty.   Incestuous villain ! yield !
My sword doth guard. No more canst thou flee me
Than thou canst flee thy shadow, which is Death.

  ANTONIO. My brain is fire, and every thought a
    flame,
Whose flickering forked tongues do burn and smite
As the foul kisses of some leprous bride.
I cannot follow thy loud storm of words ;
Go hence, leave me, to-morrow we will speak.

  ORISINO. Draw sword, defend thyself, and yield
    her me.
I come not here with fair and specious words,
But drunken with my hate's fierce fumes, and with
Plain passion, that doth seek its ends by straight,
Not crooked path.

  ANTONIO.   Thy wandering windy words

Do drift their way but slowly thro' the sense,
And I have neither strength nor will to seek
Their meaning.　Go; my brain is in a whirl
Of trouble-tost tempestuous thoughts.　Begone!

ORISINO (*advancing*).　Defend thyself, if thou
　　would'st seek to save
Thy venemous life, or I will tread thee out
Like crawling reptile.

ANTONIO.　　　　　I scarcely fathom yet
What thou dost will.　Why seekest thou to fight
With me, thy friend?　Thou art but drunk, go
　　hence!　　　　　　　　　　　　　　　[thee.

ORISINO. Liar!　I own no friendship bond with
" Defend thyself," are the last words I speak,
Until I lean hellward to curse thee there.

ANTONIO. Assuredly, I have no humour now
To bandy words with thee as thou willest.

　　　　　　　(*They fight*, ANTONIO *is killed*).

ANNIE.

O LIST, beloved, calm your tremulous heart,
Your tears are vain, you will forget full soon;
Love is but like a sensual, sweet tune
That stills the sense; for when the last notes part,
We wake to consciousness with a faint start.
The love birds pair and build again in June,
And weave new dreams beneath a latter moon.
Courage, 'tis but a momentary smart.

Your lips are sweet, and your sad face as fair
As pale white rose that blooms into a red;
And those curled locks of hyacinthine hair,
That drape in golden fleece thy neck and head,
Still hold my sense and heart within their snare
Though destiny another word has said.

My heart is like a crystal filled with tears,
That the least breath will break. Speak not a word,
For each doth pierce me like a sharpened sword
That quickens in the sense.   My open ears
Hear but the sighing sound of stricken fears,
And my eyes see but ghosts who lean meward
Wringing their hands.   Too weak am I, O Lord!
To bear the burden of the looming years.

I dare not raise my face to look at ye,
Ye years still dreaming in futurity,
Ye barren days and fruitless nights unborn.
The dark wall of the present is too steep—
No gleam of sun or moon therein doth creep—
And veils a night that ne'er will look on dawn.

Nay, think it not so hard, I loved you well
And even now I will aver that love
Still lives.   Nay, gaze not so like wounded dove,
But kiss me, sweet, before we say farewell.
God wot, it was not my unguided will
That led me to the altar.   My soul was rife
With grief when my lips spoke the name of Wife,
For I loved you and love you even still.

Nay, do not weep.   Nay, clasp your hands not so.
Your grief is mine, your sorrow is mine own,
And wrings my soul with the like suffering.
Come, Annie, kiss me once before I go,
And think of me when sitting here alone,
As I of thee, though life may sigh or sing.

My sweet, kill me not so, but lay the steel
    Against my heart.
Fear not, I will not cry, I will not feel
    Nor even start.

I will but clasp and kiss thee till I die;
    It will be worth
More than my life, for I shall know that I
    Kept thee till death.

And if thou wilt, then lay me in some place
    Where thou must pass
Often, and cull the flowers that interlace
    Amid the grass.

I shall be happy; they will be from me
    An offering,
And whisper, sweet, the love I keep for thee
    All blossoming.

Believe me, Annie,
  'Tis want of money
That forces us apart :
  It is not any
Capriciousness of heart.
  Pity me, Annie.

Believe me, Annie,
  There are not many
Truer loves on earth than mine ;
  Flowers in a cranny
Of desert wall must pine.
  Pity me, Annie.

It is weary regretting,
There is no forgetting
    Of sorrows.

Come days and come nights,
Ye bring undelights
    And morrows.

Come winter and spring,
No summer can bring
    Me gladness.

Come months and come years,
Ye bring me new tears
    Of sadness.

Yet beneath and above,
Float the spirits of love
    Condoling.

And when they have passed,
Death comes up at last
    Consoling.

How sweet it is to lie
Amid the soft cool grass,
And watch the evening sky
Change grey, and changing pass.
I listen to the drowsy bee
And wonder what are we;
I listen to the stream,
It murmurs like a dream;
And listlessly I linger
Weaving with busy finger
These varied flowers into
A wreath of varied hue;
And as I weave, I throw
Into the stream below
The flowers I refuse,
As men throw the love they use.

Some how it happeneth
They weave a fairy wreath,
The basil and mignonette,
The rose and the violet,
The graceful eglantine
With the scented jessamine,
And hundred other buds
Entwine within the floods.
Now all the flowers lie
Opposed harmoniously,
And seem to glide and dance
In love and radiance ;

One flower alone is left
Within my lap bereft;
It is the sorrowing aloe
Crowned with unearthly halo
Of a hundred weary years;
I will water it with tears
And place it in my bower,
For I am an aloe flower,
And sisters we will be,
Peaceless and sorrowful we.

The ground is sparkling bright with dew,
The stars bathe in the silent stream,
The moon a light white, green, and blue,
Thro' every copse and glade flings through,
And nightingales dream a singing dream
      That fills the skies
With sad sweet harmonies.

The trembling odorous air is filled
And overlaid with too much sweet ;
The wandering breeze is almost stilled,
Like a girl whose passion's rage has killed
All consciousness, save love's sweet heat.
      Love doth present
To all his sacrament.

The castle is black against the sky,
Sleep reigns in every room save one,
But sitting in the garden, I,
Without a tear, without a sigh,
Watch like a calm-eyed sphinx of stone
   That window's light,
Where passes a bridal night.

I watch the moon with a steadfast eye,
    She glides like a ghost away
Thro' long unending reaches of sky
    That seem like an azure bay;
Half veiled in a veil of spray
    In a swoon she is gliding by.

I follow her course with weary brain,
    Unheeding the thoughts that sigh,
For I am tired of pleasure and pain,
    And only long to die,
To sleep with no dream nigh,
    Where love and longing are twain.

My body wet with dew,
  I shiver on the stair;
The wind is wandering thro'
  My fluttering dress and hair.

I turn to look again
  Upon the moon and sky;
I press my weary brain
  And hopeless long to die.

For life is but a snare,
  An empty, idle boast,
A chalice filled with care,
  A fleeting shadowy ghost.

I am almost now afraid
To climb the echoing stair,
For every rustling air,
And wandering light and shade,
Seem to be mocking me and my despair.

The oriel window there
Weaves shadows on the floor ;
The pallid moon doth stare
Right down the corridor,
Sealing with signet seal their chamber door.

Seeming to say, Beware !
His lips are not for thee,
Walk through thy life and wear
Humbly thy destiny,
Till opens imminent eternity.

ANNIE.

The door is past,
 I stand aghast,
And, with emotion pale,
 I draw the bed's white veil.

Face leaned on face,
 In last embrace
They lie in the still gleam,
 Like shadows of a dream.

Ay! she is fair,
 Cheek, lips, and hair,
She smiles within her sleep,
 As though she saw me weep.

His hands entwine
 Linkéd in thine,
Life gave him unto thee,
 But Death restores him me.

O for a heaven of singing,
   Of delight and of love,
Where all the heavens are ringing
   Beneath and above,   [dove.
With music as soft as the light of the wings of a

Where roses for ever are blooming
   'Mid myrtles and vine,
Where stars and moon are illuming
   The bowers where twine
The mystical eons, the glory of vision divine.

Where breezes for ever are sighing
   Their love to the stream,
Whose murmur is ever replying
   Like a dream to a dream,
Whose harmony wanders as fitful as wind-driven
   gleam.

Where passion and love never dwindle ;
　　Where love is not lame ;
Where delights for ever enkindle
　　And pass into flame,　　　　[they came.
In splendours undying, for dying they come as

Where there is delight and no sorrow
　　'Tween the bud and the fruit ;
Where there is no past and no morrow,
　　Where the spirit is mute
Listening sadly to dreams between music of harp
　　and of lute.

All this I can give to thee, dearest,
　　This fire will give death.　　　[fearest
Breathe, therefore ; the fumes that thou
　　Are sweeter than breath,　　[than earth.
For they will give death and death is sweeter

Shadows and lights wax dimmer,
Shaping a mystic glimmer,
    A gloom of sullen red ;
The air grows heavy and thicker,
The lamplights tremble and flicker,
    In the darkling and dead
    Vapours that spread.

Between the mists unfolden,
Unto mine eyes beholden,
    Pale phantoms lean to me ;
Their hands for pity reaching,
Their voices grace beseeching ;
    I see them pass and flee
    Sorrowfully.

How fair his face doth seem
Beneath the white moonbeam,
Like a sweet passing shape within a passing dream.
Oh! vase of burning tears
Bound in the frost of years,
Break now thine icy chains for the dawn of a new
day nears.

The morn is breaking now,
Around, above, below,
Winnowing the white clouds as wind doth winnow
snow.
Brow bound with golden plumes,
The sun again illumes
The orange widening sky, and Day his reign
assumes.

A long, white shroud of light
Is spreading o'er the Night,
And all her raven tresses are turning gold and
bright;
My dress I throw away,
For, sinless now, I may
Intwine my limbs in thy dispassionate cold clay.

The night's dark race is run,
Day is not yet begun,
And side by side we lie the dead by the living one.
Oh! hail, Oh! hail, Oh! hail,
Deliverance cannot fail,
Life closes her weary life at last, so weak and
pale.

We shall wake to laugh or weep,
We shall know if death be deep,
Or we shall sleep perhaps a calm and dreamless
sleep,
And men will shed their tears,
Aye, for a million years,
Till each in turn his burden lays at this goal of
fears.

BERNICE.

To B——.

PALE in moonlight glistening
  Water lilies lie,
I at window listening
  Hear the fountain warble
  Softly to the marble,
  Breathing to the sky
  Echoes of a cry.

Upon the purple bosom of the night
The moon is dreaming softly, she doth seem
Like a pale beauty languidly reclining
Amid rich silken cushioned canopies.

F

The winds are hushed, no breeze disturbs the scene,
Only the warbling of the fountain's song
And the full molten murmur of a bird
The silver silence break with melody.
The sultry air is filled with rose perfume
And soft-shed scent, whose wings up-bear my soul
Higher than wildest music ever flew,
Into a heaven where mystic chords unite
Shadow with heat, the day unto the night.
Here in this garden, thro' the odorous summer
I dream with many yearnings in my heart,
Strange bitter blossoms born of tears and fire,
Whose passionate and sweet solicitudes
Feed vulture-wise upon my bloodless life
Of sleepful vigils, and short starting sleeps,
And famine-smitten nights of impotence,
And hungering days yet knowing no desire.
Here in the shadow of the purple roses

I listen to the fountain murmuring
Softly, O softly, to the water lilies,
The secret of Bernice. I see her face
Arise from out the blanching water flowers,
Her face of white rose, gazing on me sadly.
O would I might forget, but when I hearken
Unto this fountain's mazy murmuring,
I fain would hear her story, none is listening,
The old sad tale of Bernice and the lilies,
No one is listening, all is silent here.
Yea, I can tell it softly, breathe it low,
In under voice to this sweet purple rose.

One summer night, ah ! years have passed since then,
I sat by Bernice 'neath the oriel window,
Drinking the dreamy splendour of the moon
And the delirious perfumes of the night,
Till in my feverish veins the blood took fire,

And love fell sick with famine for her face.

I held her feet between my hands, and laid

My head between her knees, and gazed upon

Her downward-gazing eyes in ecstacy.

I wound the heavy tresses of her hair

Across my face and tried to weep: passion

Had dried my tears, life longèd unto death.

The demon of her destiny then spoke:

" The night is fair, let us stray down the garden,

And sit beside the fountain where the lilies

Lie gazing on the moon.   It will be sweet

To bathe by night."   With linkéd hands we went

Unto the tiny lake of fountain born,

And bathed unwatched amid the flowers.

She was a vision of voluptuousness,

And o'er the water streamed her wondrous hair

Like braids of gold, she standing bosom-deep

Leaning from out the silver gleaming wave,

The love of all my years came over me,
A fiery breath, and all my thoughts and dreams
Took fire, those unreaped fields of vision were
But one flame burning in that instant hour.
Her lips were fast upon my face, I gazed
Within the vaporous languors of her eyes
Until love's burden grew intolerable.

I know not ho   it was, her kisses stung,
Her bird-like throat full-filled with fluttering voice
Leaned over me, and all her sultry hair
Fell round my face.   The perfume of the roses
Drove me mad.   I know not how it was,
In kissing her, I held her face beneath
The pallid water-flowers, until it grew
More wan than they.   The roses were asleep,
The moon saw not between the darkling trees,
Only the lilies saw her drownèd face.

And now through all the odorous summer night
I hearken to the fountain's warbling song,
Murmuring softly, O softly, to the lilies
The secret of Bernice, my only love.

Pale in moonlight glistening
Water lilies lie,
I at window listening
Hear the fountain warble,
Softly to the marble,
Breathing to the sky
Echoes of a cry.

SONNET.

NIGHT PERFUME.

THE sky is one bare blank, one sheet of lead,
Without a star or cloud.   Low laid the moon
O'er dark dim trees floats like a gold balloon ;
No breeze doth sigh, a silence still and dead
Hangs like a raiment round the fair night's head.
Even the fountain's weary warbling tune
Tells us of quiet.   With orange odours strewn,
And rose-shed scent the breathless air is spread.

We listen to the night, the gleaming meadow
Is filled with long bright lines of light and shadow
And glitters like the sea.   Her balmy breath
Falls on my cheek, and in the mystic gloom
Of silk and muslin filled with her perfume,
I lay my head, and dream that love is death.

RONDO.

Did I love thee? I only did desire
To hold thy body unto mine,
And smite it with strange fire
Of kisses burning as a wine,
And catch thy odorous hair, and twine
It thro' my fingers amorously.
  Did I love thee?

Did I love thee? I only did desire
To watch thine eyelids lilywise
Closed down, and thy warm breath respire
As it came thro' the thickening sighs,
And speak my love in such fair guise
Of passion's sobbing agony.
  Did I love thee?

Did I love thee ? I only did desire
To drink the perfume of thy blood
In vision, and thy senses tire
Seeing them shift from ebb to flood
In consonant sweet interlude,
And if love such a thing not be,
      I loved not thee.

BALLAD OF A LOST SOUL.

ONE night a ghost laid hands on me,
  The dernful spirit of my dream,
And led me wandering o'er the sea,
  A sea divided by a gleam.
The wind scarce moved the burnt black heath
  On dry cliff's edge, the fluctuant tide
In green foam-whitened waves beneath,
  Curled low against the steep rock's side.

He sate me on a narrow ledge,
  And at my feet he lay him there,
I could not flee, upon the ridge
  Of life he held me.   In despair
I took my soul from out my heart,
  And flung it from me without care,
Skyward it flew like bow-shot dart,
  Or wrist-cast hawk that springs in air;

Then, swooping into sudden sight
  On straightened wings across my eyes,
Then wheeling, fled from left to right
  Sailing incessantly the skies;
Thro' pathless wastes of heaven unknown
  My soul did wander thus in fear,
Seeking the yet unrisen sun,
  Not knowing whither side to steer.

And sitting on the dusky height
   Over the moon-unbeaconed sea,
I watched my soul's unguided flight
   In terror and expectancy;
Until a star arose above
   The long wall of the green sea line,
I knew it was the planet of love
   By its cold crescent crystalline.

Astarte-ward my soul then fell,
   Beyond the light of Love's bent face,
Like passing star, from heaven to hell
   Adown the interlying space;
Betrothed unto new bridal bed
   A bought slave kissed, and drugged, and sold,
Poppy and red rose chapleted,
   Cheek filleted and robed in gold.

The demon still glares in mine eyes,
　　Stretched lying at my pale weak feet,
He counts on finger tips my sighs,
　　And keeps my tears.　　He laughs a sweet
Low laugh within my stricken ears,
　　And leads me weeping in control
Along this shore whose waves are tears,
　　Until his shadow grows my soul.

SONNET.

THE CORPSE.

WONDERING I gaze upon each lineament
Defaced by worms and swollen in decay,
And watch the rat-gnawed golden ringlets play
Around the sunken outline, shrivelled, bent
In hideous grimace.   The bosom rent
Is opening rose-like 'neath the sun's warm ray,
And Nature, smiling on the new-born May,
Doth own this corpse a part of her intent.

I try to lift it from the ground, but lo,
The poor head falls.   A locket thus detached
Lies in my hand ; fear seizes hold on me,
I gaze upon it, trembling, for I know
The trinket well, one word thereon is scratched,
I read, and, bending, kiss her reverently.

A PAGE OF BOCCACE.

A CRIMSON light, all faint with delight,
　　Steals thro' my lady's room,
And the scented air is moved by the rare
　　Songs spun in the mystic loom
Of canaries' throats, whose untaught notes
　　Float thro' the glimmer and gloom.

Dreaming she lies with fast closed eyes
　　Within the dim alcove,
As I bend over her she seems to stir
　　With the instinct of my love,
For down the streams of her drifting dreams
　　I may be the spirit above.

The breath from her mouth is like air from the south,
   It kisses my face and eyes,
And the touch of her hair which falls everywhere
   In restless harmonies,
My spirit doth wake to joys that break
   In a broken song of sighs.

She is bathed in the deep dream-mist of sleep
   Guided by love's faint ray,
In her lap's soft bed lies a book half read,
   A book I read yesterday;
It tells how human is soft sweet woman,
   How her love doth pass away.

* * * * * *
* * * * *

I gently took from her lap the book
   And opened it at the place
That she waking might see how erringly
   A woman may run in love's race;
I awoke not her, but without a stir
   I dreamingly kissed her face.

SONNET.

THE SUICIDE.

LYING upon these slimy stones, I peer
Down in the inky tank of lonesome well,
Where never mirrored morn or star did dwell:
No nightingale from cypress covert near
The heavy hanging solitude doth cheer,
Only a hooting owl is audible,
Passing on silent wing he wails my knell,
Seeming to have divined what led me here.

Leaning I drink—this well I take for grave,
Afar from prying ken in one black night,
Unhallowed by a foul religious rite
My bleaching bones will lie in dernful wave,
For wolves and ravens would I hail to me,
Sooner than man's detested sympathy.

SERENADE.

THE infidel has no heaven,
  The Christian has but one,
Whilst I, fairest Queen! have seven,
  Each singly wooed and won.
Thy heart, O most soulful treasure!
  Thine eyes, limpid hazes of light.
Thy mouth, O most tuneful measure!
  Thy cheeks, roses red and white.

Sweet bosom, the sweetest and fairest,
  All given, all yielded to me.
Sweet body, the sweetest and rarest
  Surrendered, belonging to me.
But as night would be lonesome and dreary
  If star-eyes gazed never down,
So these would be loathsome and weary,
  Uncrowned with womanhood's crown.

SONNET.

The Lost Profile.

Just like a pale white sea-shell misted rose
Is her small ear, and o'er her shoulders fair,
Like trailing hyacinth, flows the clustering hair;
And column-wise straight from her bosom grows
The large full throat.   Upon a gold ground glows
The half-lost face; the shadows deepening where
Lie unbeholden beauties, and her bare
Sweet arms an open vesture hiding shows.

Like this reverted head are memories:
For gazing on the past the dreamer sees
A vision of dead faces turned from sight,
Between the glooms of shadow-shapen night
Dimly pourtrayed; for blinding years reveal
Them unto us only in lost profile.

SONG.

LOVE gazed on sweet beauty, and said :
"Oh ! there, I might pillow my head,
And dream o'er the love that is dead."

Love laid on the virginal bed
And kissed the rose breast blossoms red
Till the beauty faded and fled.

Love rose with his pinions outspread,
Forgetting the weak heart that bled,
For Love is by loveliness led.

SONNET.

UNATTAINED.

I SAT beside a wondrous apple tree,
Whose branches were on every side weighed down
By rich and luscious fruit, some red, some brown,
Some pink, some white, all colours one could see.
The ripening fruitage stirred a thirst in me,
So, pulling one, I ate, but with a frown
Threw it aside ; taste, colour both had flown,
Like dreams when gazed at through reality.

I plucked and ate until my taste was gone,
Then, viewed them with contempt. At last, one day
I spied upon a topmost twig a fair
Fruit which hung out against the sky alone,
I climbed and climbed, but out of reach it lay,
Till it fell withered grey from sun and air.

THE BALCONY.

O MISTRESS sweet !   O mine ! mistress adorable !
Thy memory doth shine thro' years unfathomable,
Paling all lesser loves, as Venus when she flies
Forth like a new-fledged dove athwart the starry
     skies.
I see thee in my dreams upon thy balcony,
Drinking the pale moonbeams, lost in a reverie ;
As when I watched thine eyes and sang an under
     tune,
And all the southern skies seemed purple diamond
     strewn.
I see thee as thou wast upright majestical,
Thy full arms falling crost, and shadows mystical
Playing around thy face, that purely Greek profile
Of tender subtle grace as taken from a seal.

Art thou as fair as then, O thou! my mistress
    sweet !
Ah! I did know thee when kings knelt around thy feet,
When gold was spilt as water, when death was
    sought and found
For thee sin's fairest daughter, for thee love's
    empress crowned.

Is all now gone and passed ?   Is all now wrecked
    in dust ?
Cannot a kingdom last ruled by the sceptre lust;
Have men set now above thee another, a younger
    queen ?
Are there none now to love thee ?   Thy lovers who
    have been ?
Is all thy beauty dead ?   Has ravening decay
Seized on thy peerless head and streaked its gold
    with grey ?

May be!   All things must pass, yet gazing in my
    dream
I see thee in its glass mirrored as in a stream,
Unchanged thou sleepest there tho' time doth fly
    so fleet,
Untouched by grief or care, impassionate and sweet.
If I should meet thee now, could I love as before?
A something whispers " No," within my ear, " No
    more.
For no man sinks to sleep and dreams his dream
    again,
A dream awakes to weep, and joy once past is
    pain."

SONNET.

LOVE'S GRAVE.

WHEN the day of thought has passed I stray around
A sweet, retired grove, bedecked with flowers
Of widowhood ; there are the tranquil bowers
Whose calm is never broken by a sound
Or echo from the world ; there all is crowned
With still sad peace.   So in the secret hours
Thither I turn my thoughts and weep fresh showers
Of love upon that verdant spot of ground.

What men call pleasure I have known, yet here
When all the bitter feast is o'er, I come
To kneel and pray and live within the year
That long has passed.   It is my stricken home,
And sitting by its fireless hearth, I hear
Sad memories wail like night-winds round a tomb.

SERENADE.

I HAVE wandered to my love
When the stars kiss in the sea,
When the breeze doth sigh above
In a love-taught melody ;
I have wandered to my love
As the moth does to the light,
As the thrush does to the grove,
As the day does to the night.

Like the songs of hollow shells,
Or the music of a stream ;
Like the murmur of sea swells,
Or the dreaming of a dream,
I do sing to her I love,
For the spirits guiding me
All my songs and dreamings move
By ineffable decree.

SONNET.

SUMMER.

THE tedded grass breathed fragrance of crushed thyme,
The swan seemed slumbering on the silent wave,
And linnets from the flowerful closes gave
Forth sweetly songs in sad uncadenced rhyme,
The setting sun unspeakable, sublime,
Gazed like a god ; and down the blue concave,
Like nun adoring in cathedral nave,
The wan moon lay, awaiting her full time.

Drinking the rich deep music nature sang
I sat in dream, lost in a reverie
Of sound ; for in a sweet possessive pang
The clear tones of the wondrous melody
Throughout my spirit rapt in worship rang
Hushing the pain of every memory.

SONNET.

Laus Veneris.

I AM most lovely, fair beyond desire :
My breasts are sweet, my hair is soft and bright,
And every movement flows by instinct right :
Full well I know my touch doth burn like fire,
That my voice stings the sense like smitten lyre ;
I am the queen of sensuous delight ;
Past years are sealed with the signet of my might ;
And at my feet pale present kneels a buyer.

My beds are odorous with soft-shed scent,
And strange moon flowers a tremulous twilight air
Weave over all ; and here, alone I sing
My siren songs, until all souls are bent
Within the subtle sweet melodious snare.
God, making Love, made me Love's grievous sting.

RONDEL.

LADY! unwreath thy hair
  That is so long and fair,
May's rain is not so sweet
  As the shower of loosened hair
  That will fall around my feet.
Lady! unwreath thy hair
  That is so long and fair.

The golden curls they paint
  Round the forehead of a saint
Ne'er glittered half so bright
  As thy electric hair:
  It pales the morning's light.
Lady! unwreath thy hair
  That is so long and fair.

Lady! unwreath thy hair
  That is so long and fair,
And weave a web of gold
  Of thy enchanted hair
  Till all be in its hold.
Lady! unwreath thy hair
  That is so long and fair.

SONNET.

In Church.

From flowerful fields where a full summer glowed,
Calm with the passion of our love, we strayed
Into an antique chapel, where has prayed,
Since centuries, the peasant to his God :
Silence there reigned, in reverence we bowed
Before the altar.   Thro' stained windows played
The red sunset, until with light and shade,
Purple and gold, the whole was overflowed.

'Tis there in sorrow time the crowds toil-tired
Seek consolation in their misery ;
The stricken heart whose way is difficult
There leaves the burden of the thing desired,
And goes forth calm, with those mild hopes that see
Beyond the bitterness of things occult.

SONNET.

SUMMER ON THE COAST OF NORMANDY.

THE wind takes breath and softly sighs its sigh
Thro' her fair fragrant hair.   By sea-beach here
We listen to a music sad to hear,
That pours its soul from out the earth and sky
In one long lingering, loving melody.
The ocean waves are still, the sky is clear.
Buds blossom in the mild moist atmosphere
And Nature joys in her fecundity.

We see not Love; we only feel presence
Of something hovering yet invisible;
Not in the sight nor ear, but in the sense
Are his wings seen, and his voice audible,
A fragmentary music, whose intense
Tones find no words its secret soul to tell.

H

A NIGHT OF JUNE.

THE night was drowned
And crowned
With over-much delight ;
A breathless heat
Too sweet
Made faint the sense and sight.

Hanging between
The green
Of vine inwoven bower,
A plenilune,
In swoon,
Glowed like a golden flower.

The shadows slept
        And crept
Like fairies to and fro;
    And roses hung
        And swung
Their censers high and low.

    Her gleaming breast
        Was dressed
In clouds of amber hair;
    And her breath came
        Like flame
Thro' the deep moon-lit air.

Her arms were wound
Around
My downward-gazing face ;
And lips reposed,
And closed
Close kissing on the place.

Till passion's ache
Could take
No new breath to respire ;
But sank to sleep
In deep
Visions of blind desire.

Our souls were filled,
    And stilled
With weight of heavenly tears,
    And sacred, glad,
    And sad
Unreachable strange fears.

    " Oh ! misery !
      Ah ! me ! "
She murmured o'er and o'er,
    " This night will pass
    Alas !
As other nights before."

The moon doth bathe
Her path
In liquid light and splendour;
As even so
Doth glow
My soul with love most tender.

Life gives us gleams
In dreams
Of something in swift flight,
An instant star
Afar
Lost in the deeps of night.

Joy and delight
Are bright
Only a short-lived hour ;
And day 's too soon
In June,
And love 's too frail a flower.

SONNET.

La Charmeuse.

Come hither to my bosom, subtle snake,
And lie within my breasts; I fear no harm,
For us in spell a weird magnetic charm
Twain turns to one.   My shuddering senses ache
On passion's bitter bound ; strange dreams I slake
In kissing thee.   Sleep on ! what doth alarm
Thee, O my sweet ?   Is not my bosom warm ?
Lie still, the hour is not yet come to wake.

Thy long lithe length entwines around my throat
In strong voluptuous coils ; I watch thee float
Leaned out in air to strike the frightened dove,
Thy body oscillates, thy jet eyes glare
Lurid with fire.   Oh ! fly the circling snare
Bewitchéd bird, for here is death in love.

SONG.

THE ASSIGNATION.

DRINKING the warm rich air
Laden with breath of roses,
I leaned and kissed her fair
Sweet bosom and her hair
Within the laurel closes.

The purple skies were strewn
With stars innumerable;
And in love-laden swoon
Upon Night's breast the moon
Lay half invisible.

Till, lo ! Astarte bright
Rose o'er the shadowy vale,
And filled the whole deep night
With crystalline low light,
White, tremulous, and pale.

Then on the star-lit bank,
Dreaming of what love's bliss is,
We trembled and we sank;
And thro' her lips I drank
Her soul in rapturous kisses.

SONN T.

To a Lost Art.

Gone from me, dead, O child of my weak heart!
Child, yet a mistress, wooed most lover-wise,
Wooed long,—but never won,—with weary sighs,
With toil and many tears; but tho' we part
For e'er I love thee still; I now must start
Upon another path, with other eyes
And hands to beckon me.   Will they despise
Me as thou didst? my sweet, my own lost Art.

Tho' I have wed thy sister, thou, my sweet
Wilt keep thy place in my most hidden sense;
My dreams and secret thoughts will ever pour,
Not gifts of tribute shells around thy feet,
But love's sad offering of my impotence,
A fruitless wave that can but kiss thy shore.

HENDECASYLLABLES.

ELIANE.

HERE is absolute love-time, hear me, Carmen,
Carmen, fairest of women, we are lovers,
Lovers such as the dreaming senses vision
In those luminous moments of immortal
And full mystical blisses where the soul is
As a blossom in summer's burning noontide.
Here we wandering through the gardens moon-lit,
And faint bowers of odour laden roses,
Sing songs womanly speaking sweetest passion,
Such as Lesbians, over-smitten lyres
Kissing sister-ward leaning o'er the chosen,
Sung to feverish under-tunes in list'ning
To the fluctuant breathing of the ocean.

CARMEN.

Leaving suppliant lovers (who are falser?)
Beyond hearing of their bewailing.   Within
Pale place, beautiful, full of fairest flowers,
In low glimmering of the fading twilight
Lying, hand upon hand we kissing softly,
Watching moon risen through the starless heaven,
Slowly burn to a fireless cinder pleasure.

SONG.

My soul is like a house of doves,
　Each day desires depart,
The doves return, but the desires
　Return not to the heart.

The azure of the sky is paled
　Beneath their flocks in flight,
That, passing, seek from star to star
　A refuge for the night.

O haste! my dream, or thou wilt find
　An empty nest in May,
Only the down and broken shells
　Of the birds flown away.

LE SUCCUBE.

List well! I went towards a wood
By night when all was solitude.

There I surprised mine Enemy
In dark hair sleeping tranquilly.

She smiled amid the rippling deep
Of her dark hair, her eyes asleep.

"That smile by some cruel mystery
Thou hast despoiled from me," said I,

"And thou dost sleep, assuaged fiend,
The sleep that thou from me did'st rend!"

And then I killed the Enemy
In dark hair sleeping tranquilly.

Her fatal blood flowed here and there
Over the barren briars bare.

Her fatal blood amid the closes
Dishonouréd the white snow roses.

You have drunk up her life, O flowers!
From whom exude strange tears in showers.

The sombre purples of her wound
Shine in the clustering roses round.

Oh! could I fly your sight beyond,
Red flowerage of this rocky mound.

But the Charm with her sullen blisses
Re-lives in these flower chalices.

The languors of the ancient taint
Weigh heavy in their odours faint.

O conquered heart! thou hast no hope
To quit the coverts of the slope

Of this vast wood.   O heart exiled,
Bewitched by roses and beguiled!

(Translated from the French of Catulle Mendès).

I

A SAPPHIC DREAM.

I LOVE the luminous poison of the moon,
The silence of illimitable seas,
Vast night, and all her myriad mysteries,
Perfumes that make the burdened senses swoon
And weaken will, large snakes who oscillate
Like lovely girls, immense exotic flowers,
And cats who purr through silk-enfestooned bowers
Where white-limbed women sleep in sumptuous state.

My soul e'er dreams, in such a dream as this is,
Visions of perfume, moonlight and the blisses
Of sexless love, and strange unreachéd kisses.

PAGAN POEMS.

BY

GEORGE MOORE.

LONDON:

NEWMAN AND CO,

43, HART STREET, BLOOMSBURY, W.C.

—

MDCCCLXXXI.

CONTENTS.

PAGAN POEMS.

À

I. d'A.

À TOI que je désire, à toi qui m'a quitté,
J'offre ces quelques vers à défaut des caresses
D'autrefois, car, hélas! Maîtresse des maîtresses,
Je porte encore en moi ta superbe beauté.

Je t'ai tendu la main, demandant charité,
Et tu m'as prodigué des jours dont les richesses
M'ont brisé, des moments pleins de chastes tristesses,
Qui remplirent mon cœur de divine clarté,

C'est pourquoi, voyant bien que jamais de ce monde
Je ne baiserai plus ta tête folle et blonde,
Je donne à ton image un durable séjour,

Car tu liras ton nom sur les premières pages
De ce pauvre roman, qui parle de l'Amour
Mourant dans les lits clairs et les noirs sarcophages.

𝕾𝐨𝐧𝐧𝐞𝐭.

—

SPLEEN.

THE room is quiet, the fire flickers and burns,
A heavy silence stagnates in the air.
No hate, no love, no hope and no despair,
Nothing: I read and write and think by turns.

Repulsive, inessential sorrow yearns
And looks within mine eyes; the oil lamp flares,
The portrait of my mistress strangely stares,
A few rich flowers are fading in their urns.

Will this go on for ever?   Shall I die
One day? I wonder what I'll be when old?
The moon is slowly wandering through the sky.

SPLEEN.

Oh! dreamt-of mistress lovely to behold,

But alas! lost in perfect purity,

Is there no sin to cheer my heart grown cold?

ODE TO A BEGGAR GIRL.

THROUGH the crowded city,
Through the tranquil town,
Pale and passionless you wander,
Holding, as the Virgin holds the Child
In the first Italian masters,
Your neglected baby
Pressed against your breast.

There is something awful in your dark
Look of woe beyond mere sorrow;
Now you seem to me
Sorrow typified incarnate, yea,
Girl, you pass across my dreams
Like a wraith before a festival,
Startling joy to grief.

You are very wonderful !

There is something sphinx-like in your face,

Something mystic in its mournfulness

That oppresses me.

Who are you, and what are you ?

Were you born of parents like yourself ?

Were you nursed upon a bosom

Like the wretched infant who is sleeping

Now amid the rags

Wrapped around your own ?

Did you never know a pleasant hour ?

Have you never had a glimpse of life ?

Did you never think it fair ?

These are dreams of fancy :

You are nothing more

Than a dirty beggar bearing

Traces, ah ! of beauty past ;

You are just as vile and commonplace

As the thousands straying

Daily though our Paris streets.
I can tell your fortune :
You will bear up still a little longer,
Struggling uselessly against your fate,
Nathless certainly the night will come—
There is no escape for you.

Just a look around, a splash, a cry,
Then, a sense of suffocation. . .
Onward flows the river
Through the night.

  * * * * *

Yea, about a month ago I walked
Quickly down the never-ending
  Rue de Rivoli,
All was grey, the city and the sky,
Coldly blew the wind across the river.
Hurrying fast along, I crossed the Pont
  Louis Philippe, there,

Facing grimly, looking down upon the river,

Stands a low and almost flat-roofed building

Called the Morgue;

Looking down upon the river like a feudal lord's

Castle watching its domain,

Stands a low and flat-roofed building

Called the Morgue.

Never had I thought before to visit

This, the refuge of the miserable,

But a drizzling rain had just begun

As I crossed the bridge,

So by chance it happened that I sought

Shelter in the Morgue—

Shelter in the porch,

Having little taste for Death.

On the wall that hides the ghastly

Spectacle within from the passer

In the street

Lay a lengthy line of photographs.

First upon the list there came a man
Forty years of age or thereabouts,
Common-looking, marked with toil;
He was swollen like a bladder;
By his side I saw what seemed a woman,—
Long and draggling tresses fell
Round her decomposèd face;
Near to her a youth,
Funnily were rolled his eyes
Upward, well cut mouth and chin,
Twenty years of age.
These amused me for a while; I stood
Pensively composing
Strange biographies until I grew
Sorely tempted to pursue the search
Farther; turning to the right I saw,
Through a long extending wall of glass,
Rows of blackest stretchers,
And a corpse covered with a rough
Piece of canvas and a jet of water

Splashing down upon its face ;
Just a look sufficed, and then I turned
Terrified to gaze around. . .

Nothing but a huge stone building
Lighted from above, divided
Into equal parts
By a lofty glass partition,
One belonging to the dead
And the other to the living.
Having satisfied mine eyes
With the general aspect of the place,
Half involuntary I turned, and leaning
Over the iron railing,
Gazed upon the corpse exposed
Unto the public view.

There she lay, a quiet-looking girl !
Heaps of copper-coloured hair
Fell around and shone against the black

Marble stretcher, trailing even on the ground:
Who was she ?
Probably a little stitcher
Cruelly deserted . . Who can tell ?
May be nothing but a light of love
Lacking clients. . . . .
Little matters ! still the world goes on
Quite unconscious of its loss.

Thus I mused until my thoughts were broken
By the sudden opening of the door—
By the opening of the deadhouse door,
And you entered :
Now I recognise you perfectly ;
You were with the warder,
You were with your children, and you looked
Just a look ! The corpse was laid
On the stretcher next the door,
Then you kissed the poor and clammy lips ;
Whilst the toddling child

Played a moment with the dripping tresses.
Sad at heart, you took the ringless hand—
Weary, if not sad at heart, you looked,—
Dropped the hand, and seemed to say Alas!
Long I lingered at the door,
Curious to see you leave the Morgue,
Curious to know if you would weep;
But you did not weep,
Very weary, simply
Looking tired of life, you left the Morgue.

Wonderful indeed it is,
Gazing on you now
Begging pennies of the pitying passer,
For an instant to conceive the strange
Chance of human destiny.
What are you? a beggar born to nothing
Save a large inheritance of woe,
Whilst a dilettanti poet I
Gratify the febrile whim

Born of pampered flesh and intellect.
Either form of pleasure is a book
Never to be read by you, methinks
None could teach you either alphabet,
Still it matters little.—Say
Every life is hopeless when we think
Who will know that we have lived
In a hundred years?

Night is falling o'er the city fast,
Beggar girl, I bid you now farewell;
Catch I throw a penny passing on,
Taking up the thread of broken thoughts,
Pleasant thoughts of pleasure,
Friends, and happy hours;
Yet before I leave you I would add
Just a parting word—a last
Word of pity and advice.

" Life," you say, " is hard to bear."

Every day it will grow harder,

Pluck up courage and escape

All this misery and woe :

Death is always kindly,—die !

Think how beautiful your sister looked,

Made angelical with peace,

When she lay extended on the black

Marble stretcher in the Morgue.

Life ignores you,

You are useless,—

You were black-balled out of life,

There is nothing for you here,

Nothing,—only Death !

Follow her example and escape,

She is absolutely clay—

Common clay that gives us worms and flowers,

Flowers that nourish, worms that change again,

Insects ever seeking higher forms,

Animals extending up to Man,

Man aspiring, reaching up to God !

Ever changing, changing ever,
Wandering through the universe
In a long progressive dream,
Till at last the living clay becomes
Once again incarnate
Of the soul of man becoming God.
Life is but a dream,
And creation but a book of dreams.
Centuries hence, a million centuries hence,
You will dream again the dream of life
In a world more perfect and a form more fair.

À UNE POITRINAIRE.

WE are alone ! listen, a little while,
And hear the reason why your weary smile
And lute-toned speaking is so very sweet
To me, and how my love is more complete
Than any love of any lover.   They
Have only been attracted by the grey
Delicious softness of your eyes, your slim
And delicate form, or some such whimpering whim,
The simple pretexts of all lovers,—I
For other reasons.   Listen whilst I try
And say.   I joy to see the sunset slope
Beyond the weak hour's hopeless horoscope,
Leaving the heavens a melancholy calm
Of quiet colour chanted like a psalm

In mildly modulated phrases; thus
Your life shall fade like a voluptuous
Vision beyond the sight, and you shall die
Like some soft evening's sad serenity. . .
I would possess your dying hours,—indeed
My love is worthy of the gift.   I plead
For them.

        Although I never loved as yet,
Methinks that I might love you; I would get
From out the knowledge that the time was brief
That tenderness, whose pity grows to grief,
My dream of love, and yea, it would have charms
Beyond all other passions, for the arms
Of Death are stretched to youward, and he claims
You as his bride.   May be my soul misnames
Its passion; love perhaps it is not, yet
To see you fading like a violet,
Or some sweet thought away, would be a strange
And costly pleasure, far beyond the range
Of common man's emotion.   Listen! I

Will choose a country spot where fields of rye
And wheat extend in waving yellow plains,
Broken with woodland hills and leafy lanes;
To pass our honeymoon ;—a cottage where
The porch and windows are festooned with fair
Green wreaths of eglantine, and look upon
A shady garden where we'll walk alone
In the autumn sunny evenings ; each will see
Our walks grow shorter, till at length to thee
The garden's length is far, and thou shalt rest
From time to time, leaning upon my breast
Thy languid lily face.   Then later still,
Unto the sofa by the window-sill
Thy wasted body I shall carry, so
That thou mayst drink the last-left lingering glow
Of even, when the air is filled with scent
Of flowers ; and my spirit shall be rent
The while with many griefs.   Like some fair day
That grows more lovely as it fades away,
Gaining that calm serenity and height

Of love it wanted, as the solemn night
Steals forward, thou shalt sweetly fall asleep
For ever and for ever; I shall weep
A day and night large tears upon thy face,
Laying thee then beneath a rose-red place
Where many flowers blossom, bloom, and bud,
And long thanksgiving for the certitude
That none shall know or see thee e'er again,
That no man's soul shall even hope, so vain
Would be the longing, I shall ever make.
Though time takes all things, this it shall not take,—
Remembrance; and my future years shall be
Filled with the perfume of thy memory.

A PARISIAN IDYL.

THIS is the twilight of the summer dead,
The last few days of sunny weather; all
The flowers are faded, and the autumn woods
Are filled with yellowing tones of richest brown
And russet red, and here and there have gone
To gold more brilliant than the saffron hair
Of any English maiden. Shall we take
The express that starts at twelve for Fontainebleau,
And pass a pleasant and a charming week
Together ?—and the time is opportune,
For he is shooting grouse a thousand miles
From here, and by a very lucky chance
I have at least two hundred francs to spend.
You—you never want for money since
The count, your husband's death, although he died

Leaving to you but little, nothing save
A wretched pittance, some ten thousand francs
A year.   I blame you not, for it is quite
Impossible to live in modern Paris
Upon a fortune so inadequate.
You must have horses, carriages, a house
Luxuriantly furnished and——   But nay,
'Tis pleasanter to talk of Fontainebleau.
You have not seen the grand old castle, filled
With memories of kings and queens long dead,
And where Napoleon signed the famous act
Of abdication; and no words can paint
The beauty of the park : its avenues
Of close-cut trees and lordly terraces
Broken with artificial waters, groups
Of sculpture, flights of stately marble stairs.
And then there is the forest beautiful
Of right divine.   Summer has seen decay
Of roses white and red ; and if the air
Still tastes of June, and if the skies are bright,

'Tis only of a soft reflected glow,
Shed of a summer over now and set
For ever : summer has seen decay, so come
And see the falling of the autumn leaves.

The days will pass like minutes,—we will stroll
After a pleasant breakfast through the park
And feed the greedy fish and floating swans ;
Our hands and fingers they shall lingering touch,
Breaking the bread; those tender movements half
Involuntary that lovers know : and there
Are Bouchers in the castle, pure chefs-d'œuvre
Of decorative art : how different
From all that hideousness in the opera house !
And you will bring your horses with you,—we
Will ride together through the forest, watching
The falling of the leaves : you do not know
How beautiful you are when standing whip
In hand, holding your riding habit's skirt
Over your arm, the tiny patent leather

Boots showing beneath your trousers. . . . How I love
To take the little foot and lift you right
Into the saddle! We shall ride adown
The leafy avenues, restraining tight
In hand our horses briskly cantering
Along, and quietly we shall fall to dream
That everything is fading like the leaves,
Until the sudden stopping of our steeds
Awakes us from our half-sad reveries.

And then my arm will softly pass around
Your waist, and you will backward lean your head,
And softly, silently our lips shall meet ;
And when the sunset seems to sleep amid
The distant clouds and forest, slowly we
Shall turn our horses' heads to homeward, still
Watching the falling of the autumn leaves ;
And drinking deeply, in subdued delight,
The soundless music of the underskies.
A little dinner shall be ready set

Awaiting by a sparkling bright wood fire,

And we shall dine alone : a little soup,

A bit of fish, a partridge and a roast,

A vegetable and a bunch of grapes,

And afterwards some kissing and a chat

Beside the fire, over the coffee ; then

By nine o'clock the servant shall announce

The carriage at the door.   The purple vault

Shall glisten gloriously with golden stars—

The moon shall light the world, and we shall drive

About the autumn forest, leaning close

Against each other warmly wrapped within

The rug, the long-haired wolfskin rug, your hand

In mine, reclining back upon the same

Cushion, and breathing with an equal breath

The large and infinite sweetness of the night ;

And then there shall be sweeter afterwards,

Of which I will not speak. . . . You smile, and blush,

And kiss me. . . Well, to-morrow shall we go

And pass a pleasant week together ?   Life

Is pleasant, and a very pleasant thing
It is to live, although from time to time
Its current runs vexatiously across
Love-wrecking shoals and reefs; nous aimons bien,
But still we have our trials: you are forced
To dine alone with him three times a month.
I blame you not at all—I know you must
Have horses, carriages, a pleasant house,
Those sweet superfluous necessities
Of life—no lover's kiss could compensate
For want of these; you dine three times a month
Alone with him, and at your bank you find
Paid quarterly some twenty thousand francs.
Society is quieted with balls
And parties, a charity or two, and none
Suspects, for it is done so easily—
With such simplicity. You hide with tact
As much as possible the nasty side,
And make things easy for me, and I strive
To see but little, and that little soon

Forget, for when I dine alone with you
Your kisses chase the hateful thought away
That he is paying for the wine I drink.

Come, sweetest, I will telegraph to-night
For rooms, and we will pass a pleasant week
Together, watching the falling of the leaves.

SAPPHO.

SCENE I.

An Ionic-columned room, Sappho seated amid her attendants who are engaged in completing her toilette. On one side a porphyry table with silver boxes and vases containing odours, essences, pomatums, pins, depilatories, and the little golden scissors. In the middle of the room a bronze dolphin bestridden by a Cupid, blowing from his nostrils two jets of water, one hot, the other cold, into two oriental alabaster basins, into which the women dip alternately the white sponges. Through the purple-curtained windows, between the tops of the laurels grown at the foot of the court-wall, is seen a strip of azure sky.

SAPPHO.

LAÏS, not so entwine the golden thread
Within the hair, making a single knot
Beneath the head of all the tresses. Let
Fall loosely one, to wander fitfully
Adown the shoulder. Scropas so arranged

My tresses when I posed for Venus.   Thou,
Electra, the gold hairpin ornament
Set higher, and the scent of norris root
Shed sparingly ; and thou, O Flora, bring
My lyre, for I would sing the song I made
Last night when we walked wandering by the sea.
But canst thou tell me if Megara goes
Unto the feast of Zeno ? words are said
That Hylas loves her not, and that she craves
On bended knees his pity.

FLORA.

Nought is sure !
For all her soul is given up to him
Who will not listen to her sighs and words
Of love, who turns with loathing from her kiss.

SAPPHO.

'Tis strange indeed, for sweeter than a dream
Is that pale face of hers ; her breasts are fair

And sweeter in the mouth than any rose
For scent and taste.   He must indeed be chill,
And in his veins the blood must poorly pour,
If passion flows not molten-mad between
The flesh and spirit, when her love-warmed breath
Falls faint upon his lips.

LAIS.

He loveth thee!

SAPPHO.

Poor dreamer ! his desire has nought with mine.

[SAPPHO *takes the lyre from* FLORA *and sings*.

" That man, God-like, seems to me sitting by thee,
 Who alone doth draw to him all thy passion,
  Hears thee midwhile whispering tender speaking,
    Seeing thee smiling;

" This is what my shuddering senses tortures,
 Now I see thee, beautiful, gazing on thee,

All my love-words falter to feeble nothings,
　　Broken in sighings.

" Subtle flames stray molten in liquid fires
　Through my blood-ways, blind are my eyes, and dizzy
　Are my stunned ears, deafened with sounds of murmurs
　　Swimming around me.

" Chilling dew-damps over my flesh are breaking,
　And a heart born shivering through me wanders,
　I am wan as grass in the summer places,
　　And I am dying."

　　　　　　　　　　[*Enter* HYLAS.

　　　　SAPPHO.

What ! is it thou, O Hylas, who now comes
The third time of this morn, to weep and pray
Here at my feet ?　Hylas, the well beloved,
And favoured of the Gods with gifts divine
Of loveliness ; and Hylas, art thou not
The one adored of sweet Megara, queen
Of the Hetiries ?

Hylas.

Sappho, nay, I know
Not this, nor that, nor can I speak of aught
But one sweet word.   I come to ask
Some peace of thee; if it be Death or love
I care not : there is nothing glad in life.

Sappho.

'Tis strange and sad that thou shouldst love me thus :
Come, sit against my feet—I fain would know
For what thou lovest me.

Hylas.

Love knoweth not,
He runs with sightless eyes.   How dear it is,
Here in this doubtful light, to lie head laid
Upon thy knees, the perfume of thy flesh
Drinking, as through the textures of thy robe
It steals like wafted incense !

SAPPHO.

     Is it then
Only the sweetness of my loveliness
That from Megara turns thy love to me?

HYLAS.

I love thee as the drinker loves the wine
That maddens him—I love thee as I love
Sometimes the moon when, like a floating flower,
She swims and swoons, and fills the languid night
With luminous languors and perfumed poison'd air,
And sickening ecstacy and maddening dreams
That melt my soul like vapour into air,
And leave me chill of an unreached desire!

SAPPHO.

And when didst thou first love me?   Tell me, sweet!

HYLAS.

When first thy grave grey eyes like sunlight fell
Upon my face, the dream of dreaming dreams

Arose before me robed in sacred white
Immortally serene.   Rememberest thou,
O Sappho, the soft night we walked alone
Amid the shadows of thy garden ?   Then
Leaning to breathe the perfume of thy throat,
A pitying breeze half swept across my face
A tress of loosened hair ; within its night,
The deep luxuriant darkness of thine hair,
I saw the country of my dream : a hot
Exotic world where forests spread at large,
And mystic flowers swing their censer-cups
Across the heavy perfumed silence, where
My soul floats upward in delight as thine
Across the molten murmurs of thy song,

SAPPHO.

Thou art a strange young dreamer. Once I might
Have loved thee ; now, my love seeks other ends
Than thee.

HYLAS.

My life is as a rose within thine hand:
Thy breath like April's breeze may set its bud
On flower, or like a hard October wind
Scatter its leaves in pale flocks to the air. . .

[*Enter a slave.*

SLAVE.

Megara, the fair Samian, awaits,
To make thee homage of great offerings,
O Sappho !

SAPPHO (*to Hylas*).

She doth come to thee.

HYLAS.

I will
Go hence. . . .

SAPPHO.

Stay yet a little while, I do

Beseech.

HYLAS.

I will go hence to my despair,
And to the sorrows of a wasted life,
And mourn until the hour when death shall come
And calm these tears with sleep. I will go hence.

[*Exit* HYLAS *and enter* MEGARA *with slaves*
bearing presents.

MEGARA (*throwing herself at Sappho's feet*).

Love and fair wishes and much tenderness,
Which the immortal Gods have ever held
Higher in place than riches of the land,
I bring as a befitting crown to set
Upon the forehead of my gifts.   I lay
Here at thy feet, O Sappho, delicate robes

Of gold, by the Phœnician merchants brought
O'er many perilous miles of burning sea,
Where sultry summer hushed the slaves, back-bowed
Across the labouring oars, beyond the reach
Of the awakening lash ; these jewels once
Belonged to Princes, they were brought to me
At costly sacrifice of life, they came
From further side of desperate deserts where
Is nought but sky and yellow wastes of sand.
The wealth I lay before thee is the life
Of many nations, many provinces;
It was the meat and bread of shepherd tribes
Who drove their flocks across the mountain brows,
Living their simple life.   The fire and sword
Were loosed to prey like hordes of ravening wolves
Upon these stricken tribes, who fled their homes,
Leaving their fruitful fields and olive groves
Unto the pitiless lust of conquerors,
To live in forests and the mountain caves
Of Scythian wilderness.

Much else was done

That my fair body might not ever know

A stain or soil ; I held the world rose-wise

Between my lips, and shed its leaves in kisses.

Therefore, O Sappho, let these gifts of mine

Take new price in thine eyes, esteeming them

Beyond their value as symbolical

Of love and hate, of power and feebleness,

Of wealth and poverty, of joy and pain.

SAPPHO.

Thou hast no love for me, thou speakest words,

Fair specious words that know but little love.

Not gracious are thy offerings, since they crave

Some other gift than love for what they give.

MEGARA.

O Sappho, thou who holdest in thine hands

The cup wherein are mixed my life and death

In equal measure, veil not Pity's face,

Down throwing one against the feet of love,
Giving the other with a ruthless hand
Unto the thirsting lips of Death.   I come
Not here with words that have no faith to keep,
But with the fair outspoken simpleness
Of much o'erburdened misery that finds
No honied words to seek and beg for grace.
I ask of thee, O Sappho, but one thing,—
Thine heart has ever held it valueless.
I love young Hylas: ah ! thou knowest well
What bitterness is love; mine is a flame
That burns the very air I breathe, and like a leaf
My soul is shaken, and in every vein
Blood shivers, where the storm of my desire
Has passed, as greying spaces out at sea
Glimmer beneath the wind.   I can but cast
Myself upon the breast of dreams to find
Relief of this hard agony of love.
Give him to me, and a great wealth of love,
O'erweighing gold as feather in the scale,

Will be to thee a large inheritance,
And gratitude as guerdon wilt thou reap,
Whose over-ripened sheaves will ever pour
Sweet harvesting of love around thy feet,
And all my days will be to thee a hymn
Of thankfulness for this large-hearted love,
And unto men my tongue shall sing thy praise,
Sappho, as holiest of women.   Yea!
Thy name shall blossom, and to lute and lyre
Be sung before the altars of the Gods,
For have they not as truly righteous
Upheld but those who made much sacrifice?

SAPPHO

I often sang the bitterness of love
To thee, in words that fell between the tones
Of lyre accompaniment like star fires through
Moon-sweetened air, and after singing time,
When all my passion-lifted spirit leaned

To love, unfearing what the gods must fear,
And spoke the burden of my feverish dreams,
Thou ever didst turn with loathing and with scorn
Away, and all my prayers were but as seed
Thrown on a barren ground, that bore no fruit
But hate; and yet thou kneelest at the feet
Of whom thou ne'er didst pity.   But 'tis I,
Sappho, whom Hylas loves, and were I turned
To mercy, could I modulate and tune
The chords of his desire in harmony
With thee?

MEGARA.

Thy words are arrows barbed with flame,
That pierce my weak heart like the winter winds
The wounded fawn belated on the hills.
The Gods, in their derision, give, alas!
What joy my life beholds as fair, to thee
To waste and ruin as a worthless thing.
To-day the world is fair, for Spring o'erflows

The land with songs and blossoms, but I am wan
For him of whom my spirit dreams until
The dream becomes incarnate of delight.
I ask no gift impossible : thou hast
No love for him—then leave thy place to me
From sunset unto sunrise ; he will see
Me not, he will believe 'tis thou.   Oh, give
Me, Sappho, this imperfect night of love !

Sappho.

Askest thou death of life, or night of day ?
Delight of pain, or sweet of brine, or joy
Of grief, or fruit of sand ?   Wherefore then ask
This thing of me ?   Shall I tread pain to wine
For bridal cup, and sing my sorrow's pang
To bridal measure, and with my desire
Weave garland for another's brow ?   Take hence
These gold-spun raiments, take them hence and go !
Take hence thy wealth, and lay it at his feet,
Buying the love that thou wouldst buy of me.

MEGARA.

O Sappho! turn not with a hardened heart
Against my offerings.   I another gift
Will lay to them, and with united worth
Purchase this one thing, soul of my desire!
Here at thy feet, O cruel Sappho! I
Make unto thee my body full in flower
And perfect bloom of ripened womanhood,
As bond-slave bounden to thy plainest will,
A thing to please the pleasure of thy strange
Passion, a rose to cherish and to kill
With kisses keener than the wind or sea,
And bitter-sweet with aching softness, stung
With all the sultry perfumes of desire.

SAPPHO.

With hate and love an equal balance may
Be made whilst death be in the scale unlaid
For weight deciding.   Bow, Megara, down

Thine head, and then uplift it looking straight
Towards the ruling Gods, whom we hold high
In reverence and love, and call on them
To witness this thine oath: that when the world
Awakes fair-flushed beneath the kisses quick
Of morning, thou wilt tremble not at all,
Asking no respite, but with faithful hand
Wilt pitiless cast thy lover's life to death.
There is the dagger.   Swear thine oath to heaven!

MEGARA.

Hush, Sappho, veil thy head with mourning veil,
And humbly pray repentance of the gods,
For surely his scarce summer sun warmed life
Is not decreed in instant prime to death.
O Sappho! think of his fair face, so sweet
And softly fair, and those full fleshly limbs
Of perfect moulded grace against thee leaned,
Aweary with the wan vicissitudes

Of passion : the instinct love of womanhood
Would rise within thy breast, and thou wouldst sheath
The dagger set against his rose-white throat
And stain its snow with flush of kisses.   Why,
O Sappho ! ask of me what even thou
Couldst never do ?   I cannot give to death
The life that I would consecrate to love !
I bare my body to thee : there ensheath
The teeth and claws of passion, till I be
As dead before thee, but, O Sappho ! spare
This one sweet life !

SAPPHO.

　　　　Too pitiful is thy love :
I would do all things for a thing desired.
When once a love is no more mine, what worth
Is it to me ?   Far better see it dead
Than see it turn to loathing.   Is it not
My body's beauty that he loves ?   'Tis these
Sweet bosoms he will dream of, and not thine.

MEGARA.

O Sappho! Pity! I am weak as snow
In love's consuming hands. I am as one
Dragged onward by foul demon dreams to edge,
Divined but by the thunder-throated sea,
Of unseen precipice engulfed in night.
I cast my arms in air, but nothing reach
For help, but the loose yielding breeze.

SAPPHO.

Take this,—
Here is my dagger: it will shield thy love
Against the loathing glances of his eyes.
Thou shalt lie in my place to night, and from
The sundown to the dawning thy desire
Shall be all wholly thine; let Hylas die
In his delight,—the waking would be cruel.

SCENE II.

The sleeping chamber of Sappho, a marble-walled room divided by an immense richly embroidered curtain hanging by large rings from an iron rod, with bread-fruit ornaments at each end; against the curtain a low couch raised upon lion's claws, upon which Megara sits half reclining, gazing upon Hylas, who lies by her side in a profound slumber. Close by her hand at the head of the couch is a small tripod on cloven feet, upon it an inlaid casket with a jewelled dagger. The floor is of multicoloured marble; on the left, nearly in the middle of the room, placed on a table of a precious wood, is a female figure holding in her extended arms a mirror of polished metal. On the right is a statue of Sappho,

MEGARA.

HATH heaven aught more fair to show than this?

Sweet breast, sweet limbs, sweet hands, sweet hair.

Are they not end enough for all desire,

Though it be set with wings that darken sun

And starry throng? O Earth! most fruitful mother!

O perfect mother! Mother ever bountiful

Of gifts! What sweeter than thy lakes and streams?

What goodlier than thy sun-unfolded fields

Of sky, thy corn fields and thy sea fields hoar,

And vineyards waxing from the green to red

Fruit in their sun appointed time?   What form

Diviner than these supple moulded limbs,

These passion-parted lips, so good to kiss,

This tender throat half hidden in the hair,

And these full arms entwined around me yet?

What is there holier than thy nakedness,

Implacable relentless Venus, born

Of sea-foam and the bitterer foam of blood?

Thy shrine is built upon the world's great want,

Thy worshipper is man, and thy hands fill

The measure of his pleasure and his pain,

For thou art one with life and life is one

With thee.

SAPPHO (*heard singing outside*).

" Have not high Gods longing with loathing given,

And our sleepings woven around with dreamings

And the whole world crowned with a crown of sorrow

Filling it full with. . . .

MEGARA (*interrupting*).

The moon looks not upon the daytime yet,
But sits as a yellow-faced Egyptian queen
Filled with the languors of a southern love
Amid the purple starrèd draperies
That fold her throne.   Then why doth Sappho come?
What need the imminent hour of messenger?

SAPPHO (*continuing*).

" Thorns of passion, weakness, and fervid willing,
Hope, the green shoot grafting of weary grieving,
Love, the sense-smit shuddering of the spirit,
Weeping and laughter . . .

MEGARA.

The stars grow pale as aspen leaves, the night
Dies fast, and round her trailing garments cling
My dreams like children round a dying mother.

(looking at him)

God making thee just dreamt of woman, sweet,

Thou shouldst e'er lie head laid across my knees,

And dream adown the shifting agonies

Of Love's steep seasons, seeing the green flower catch

On red and pleasure wane to weariness,

In dreaming passing interludes of love

And weariness to pleasure wax again

In molten mood of passion's full-tide height.

SAPPHO *(singing again)*.

" Weary are they, sorrowful are their dreamings

Whom the high Gods stricken with perfect vision

Making soul-will infinite, and the senses

Mortal and weakling."

MEGARA.

The measure of thy days is meted out,

Thy sweet young life is taken as a prey,

And strangest loves are knelt to and adored

At Lesbian shrine with thee for sacrifice.

These lips will give delight to maiden mouth

No more; thine eyes will never long

And look with lingering fancies filled of love

Again; no girl will ever pass her hands and hold

Unto her languid lips this heavy hair,

Laying her head caressingly against

This cheek.   Ay, thou art verily too sweet

For death. Just here, beneath this red breast-fruit

The heart lies trembling like a fluttering bird.

Poor heart! that ne'er was mine, the dagger's point

Down-turned lies over like a hawk above

A brooding dove, thine eyes must never ope

To look on me . . . I would not see thine eyes . . .

And I will veil mine own, lest sudden fear [Death. . .

The steel's sharp point should turn aside from

Why wilt thou not look up?   Could those sweet eyes

Avert thy doom !   The dagger trembles, quick.

Courage . . . Poor heart of mine !

(She kills him.)

*   *   *   *

He shuddered once.
Yea, it is done! I can now turn my head;
He started not, no groan slipped from his lips:
Yea, he is dead; I can unveil my face,
He cannot see me now, for he is dead.

SAPPHO (*heard outside singing*).

" Through the twilight shadows of fading evening,
By the shore-strand, glimmering in the rays of
Purple sunset, purpling all the ocean
      Cliffs and the headlands.

" Women dream there, sorrowful women, dreaming,
Gazing sunward whispering sweetest secrets,
Hands on hands laid, shivering with the languors
      Born of their passion.

" Others white-robed, sister-like, wander slowly
Through the dark woods filled with the apparitions,
Mixing fearful frothing of pleasure unto
      Weeping of torments."

𝕾𝖔𝖓𝖓𝖊𝖙.

—

THE CORPSE.

WONDERING I gaze upon each lineament
Defaced by worms and swollen in decay,
And watch the rat-gnawed golden ringlets play
Around the sunken outline, shrivelled, bent

In hideous grimace.   The bosom rent
Is opening rose-like 'neath the sun's warm ray,
And nature, smiling on the new-born May,
Doth own this corpse a part of her intent.

I try to lift it from the ground, but lo!
The poor head falls.   A locket thus detached
Lies in my hand ; fear seizes hold on me,—

I gaze upon it, trembling, for I know
The trinket well; one word thereon is scratched:
I read, and, bending, kiss her reverently.

BALLAD OF A LOST SOUL.

ONE night a ghost laid hands on me,
  The sorrowful spirit of my dream,
And led me wandering o'er the sea,
  A sea divided by a gleam.
The wind scarce moved the burnt black heath,
  On dry cliff's edge, the fluctuant tide
In green foam-whitened waves beneath,
  Curled low against the steep rock's side.

He sate me on a narrow ledge,
  And at my feet he laid him there;
I could not flee, upon the ridge
  Of life he held me.   In despair
I took my soul from out my heart,
  And flung it from me without care:

Skyward it flew like bow-shot dart,
   Or wrist-cast hawk that springs in air.

Then, swooping into sudden sight,
   On straightened wings across my eyes,
Then wheeling, fled from left to right,
   Sailing incessantly the skies ;
Thro' pathless wastes of heaven unknown
   My soul did wander thus in fear,
Seeking the yet unrisen sun,
   Not knowing whither side to steer.

And sitting on the dusky height
   Over the moon-unbeaconed sea,
I watched my soul's unguided flight
   In terror and expectancy ;
Until a star arose above
   The long wall of the green sea-line,—
I knew it was the planet of love
   By its cold crescent crystalline.

Astarte-ward my soul then fell,
　　Beyond the light of Love's bent face,
Like passing star, from heaven to hell
　　Adown the interlying space ;
Betrothed unto new bridal bed
　　A bought slave kissed, and drugged, and sold,
Poppy and red rose chapleted,
　　Cheek filleted and robed in gold.

　　　.　　.　　.　　.　　.　　.　　.　　.

The demon still glares in mine eyes,
　　Stretched lying at my pale weak feet,
He counts on finger-tips my sighs,
　　And keeps my tears.　He laughs a sweet
Low laugh within my stricken ears,
　　And leads me weeping in control
Along this shore whose waves are tears,
　　Until his shadow grows my soul.

𝔖onnet.

———

CHEZ MOI.

My white Angora cats are lying fast
Asleep, close curled together, and my snake,
My many-coloured Python, is awake,
Crawling about after a two-months' fast.

The parrot screams from time to time my last
Love's name ; the atmosphere doth softly ache
With burning perfume, lazily I rake
And sift the smouldering embers of the past.

The women I have loved arise, and pass
Before me like the sun rays in a glass,—
Alice and Lizzy, Iza and Juliette ;

And some are blushing, some are pale as stone:
Heigho! The world spins in a circle yet . . .
My life has been a very pleasant one.

A LOVE LETTER.

IZA, do you remember that your sweet
   White body was surrendered to my tears?
Do you remember when I kissed your feet—
   Your dove-like feet, and then your shell-like ears?

But well we knew, alas! my own sweet lady,
That never have the stars of love shone steady.

Have you another lover?   Is his love
   Sweeter than mine, and is it what you sought?
Nay, Iza, tell me all these things, and prove
   To me the vanity of human thought.

For well I know, alas! my own sweet lady,
That never have the stars of love shone steady.

We met by common chance, as leaflet meets
   A leaflet in a wind or stream, and we
Remained together whilst the July heats
   Over the roses wafted listlessly.

But well we knew, alas! my own sweet lady,
That never have the stars of love shone steady.

You left me soon; but nay, I will not tire
   Your ears with any weak and vapourish
Lamenting, for you gave me my desire,
   You never thwarted any febrile wish.

But well we knew, alas! my own sweet lady,
That never have the stars of love shone steady.

You were so perfect that my soul should have
   In dreaming of your beauty found enough,
And carried down unto the sunless grave
   Unsullied all your many gifts of love.

But, ah ! you know, alas ! my own sweet lady,
That never have the stars of love shone steady.

If I have been not faithful, still I think
   Of you, but there have been disgraceful days,
Shameful discordant days that did not link
   The present to the holy past I praise.

But well you know, alas ! my own sweet lady,
That never have the stars of love shone steady.

For these false frailties I humbly crave
   Your fair forgiveness, for I only sinned
Because the flesh is weak, regrets will lave
   My body purer than the mountain wind.

Ah ! well you know, alas ! my own sweet lady,
That never have the stars of love shone steady.

Have you another lover ?   Tell me all,—
   Yea, even that you love him ; I can bear

To hear the worst, knowing that love must gall
   Your passions just a little, here and there.

For well I know, alas ! my own sweet lady,
That never have the stars of love shone steady.

I thank you for your love, and whilst things change,
   And men fight hard for glory, love and fame,
My thoughts shall dream, and dreaming scarcely range
   Beyond the sacred precincts of your name.

For know you not, my own, my lovely lady,
In skies of dream the stars of love shine steady ?

𝔖𝔬𝔫𝔫𝔢𝔱.

—

USED UP.

PART I.

YEA, I am sick of women, one and all ;
And thankfully I take my leave of vows
And lips and tresses, bodies, hands and brows,
For verily love tastes to me like gall.

At last I am free, and now your tiresome thrall
Is broken, and my thoughts like loosened boughs
Spring back against the light, the spirit cows
No longer, and the fleshly fetters fall.

Yea, I am sick of scent and patent leather shoes,
Silk stockings, large cravats, and jewelry,
And all this delicate life of love-abuse.

It is a weak and drivelling thing to be
The boudoir blossom that the ladies use
And then keep faded in their diary.

Part II.

A RICHMOND villa with a close-cut lawn,
A wife, a well-stocked kitchen garden lined
With fruit trees, stables and coach-house just behind,
Is certainly the prize I should have drawn

In life; indeed, I willingly would pawn
All this for that, for verily I find
Vice tiresome and stale,—my flesh has sinned
Enough.   Before the vilest lust I yawn.

I would relieve the poor when times were hard,
Amid the congregation sing the psalm
On Sundays, and attend the vestry-board.

Such seems to me a perfect dream of life,—
And then at last to die in Christian calm,
Amid my children, and my agèd wife.

LA MAITRESSE MATERNELLE.

An artist's studio.   A large room lighted from above, with
doors opening upon a garden.   A quantity of furniture in differ-
ent styles scattered over a Turkey carpet, low-cushioned seats,
deep divans, Italian cabinets and inlaid tables.   On the right a
piano draped with a rich Indian shawl ; on the left a fireplace
and small writing-table.   The walls are covered with innumerable
studies, old tapestries and mirrors.

Enter LA COMTESSE DE BEAUSAC.

THE COUNTESS.

NOT here !   But it is only two o'clock :
I said at three.   The fault is mine, or rather
My watch's.   Still I think that I will wait,
Although it be for nothing, save the joy
Of loitering through the saddest of farewells,
For I would muse and dream a moment here,

Collecting every straying memory

Upon this hour.   (*Sitting down.*)

         So all is finished now !

I was deceived in nothing, for I knew

That all would end as it has ended—nought

Was hidden from me, and I make no false

Complaint.   I loved that boy as verily

His mother never loved him.   Did I not

Assist him in his bitter poverty,

When he was friendless ?   Is not his success

Half owing to my efforts ?   With what pride

I watched each step he made, and what delight

It was to be his benefactress !

For when I knew him, years ago, he used

To work at pictures which he only sold

For sixty or a hundred francs ; I bought

Them secretly from all the dealers.   Well

I can recall to mind his studio,

High up beneath the slates : how cold it was

In winter ! and how suffocating hot

In summer ! yet it seemed a paradise
To me.   I often think of it, for there
I held him for the first time in my arms ;
And these are very sweet remembrances,
That compensate for other hateful years.
But everything must end ; and it has ended
Scarcely too soon, for verily my hair
Is filled with silver, and in three years hence
I shall be old for love ; it finished not
Too soon, for otherwise he would have learned
To loathe me.   (*Getting up.*)
              All is over now, except
To say good-bye.   I wonder where he is ?
But it is only two o'clock : I am before
My time.   (*Going to the window.*)
              How sweet the garden smells ! the sun
Is shining softly ; I will go and bid
Sadly a long farewell to all my flowers.
                         [*Exit by the window.*

Enter ALBERT DE CRÉMONT.

(*Looking at his watch.*)

'Tis half-past two; in half an hour or there-
Abouts she will be here.   I shall explain
The matter simply.   Often she has said
That lovers live to see the hour when lips
Instead of hands are given.   Why not part
To-day if we must part some day?   A chance
Is offered me to settle down in life :
I cannot marry her, and every man
Must marry—there is time for everything—
And I have loved her well these many years ;
Better perhaps than I shall ever love
Again, for she has been so very kind,
So full of sweetness for me, and the five
Delicious years of love that we have passed
Together are so many delicate chains
That bind me; every day arises now
Distinct before mine eyes, and every night,—

The parties where we danced, our walks along
The seaside, where we used to sit amid
The rocks, and in the fields; our dinners here,
The whispering and the chatting by the fire,
And then the excursion that we made last year
Through Italy.   How happy we have been!
And I am sorry all must change.   These rooms
Will soon be sold : I bid them now farewell!
There is her seat, the sofa where she used
To sit,—these cushions where she laid her head,
These chairs, these tiger-skins, this table where
She used to place her work-basket, and here
I find the book that she is reading, half
The leaves are yet uncut.   But these regrets
Are vain : there is no use in dreaming o'er
The past—the future will be pleasanter
And purer : am I not engaged to Blanche,
The only girl I ever really loved ?
Her heart is lighter than a bird, her mouth
Is redder than a rose.   How simply chaste

She seemed the other day, her brown hair loosed
Into a falling bunch that hung adown
Her dress of white muslin. She gave her hand
And spoke so sweetly, showing me her flowers
In the conservatory. I feel I love
Her—certainly I love her: who could help
Loving her innocence? and she shall be
My wife, and very soon. . . But I am still
Another woman's lover. . . Ah! how weak,
How miserably weak, how very feebly weak!
But this shall end at once.

(*Looking at his watch.*)

'Tis nearly three;
'Tis clear she is not coming here to-day,—
Then I will go to her. . . it is not quite
Five minutes' walk, not more; yes, I will go
And tell her everything. (*Going out.*)

What will she say?
She is, I think and hope, a little tired
Of me; if so, it will be easier said. [*Exit.*

Enter the COUNTESS.

Has he forgotten me ?   He cometh not,
For he is sitting by her side, and thinks
Of nothing save her presence.   She is young
And delicately simple as a flower,
And I am old. . . What bitterness is this !
My heart is aching like a wounded bird,
And I am very weary of my life,
For age is overtaking me.   Dear God !
'Tis terrible to think that there should be
No sweet returning.   If I had my youth,
How happy we might be : alas !
'Tis time that separates us.   Yes, I love
That boy, and there is nothing in the world
For me except my love !

(Going to the glass.)

But am I not
A handsome woman still ?—there are in truth
No wrinkles in my face.   What matter one,

Or two, or three grey hairs? at twenty some
Are grey.   (*Turning away.*)

      But, this, alas! is very vain.
I thought that I had crushed and trampled down
My passions, and I thought I was prepared
To bear my sorrow: I am very weak.

      (*She bursts out crying: after a pause, with
        forced calm,*)

But nay, I will be stronger: all is over;
I know it; I am reconciled, and none
Shall know I suffer.

      (*Turning over some music on the piano,*)
        What is here? His songs!
And all addressed to me. Here are the first
Verses he made for me; I love them well,
For none has ever sung them save myself.

      (*She goes to the piano and sings.*)

      " La nuit est pleine de silence,
        Ainsi qu'une immense douleur,

Et dans une douce indolence
La lune dort comme une fleur.

" Je suis ton amant, et ta blonde
Gorge tremble sous mon baiser,
Et le feu de l'amour inonde
Nos deux cœurs sans les apaiser.

" Rien ne peut durer ; mais ta bouche
Est telle qu'un fruit fait de sang,
Tous passe, mais ta main me touche
Et je me donne en fremissant.

" Douce maîtresse, écoute : J'aime
À caresser tes longs cheveux,
Et je ne vois dans le ciel même
Que ton cœur, ton corps, et tes yeux."

Enter ALBERT *hurriedly.*

Alas ! alas ! I cannot ; but indeed
It is no fault of mine—my courage failed
Me, that is all: I was determined quite
To tell her, but my resolution went,

And here I am as helpless as a child.

I do not know how everything will end,

And care but little, for I cannot change

Myself. I love that woman—that is all:

'Tis folly if you will, but it is so. . .

I know not what to do.

(*He falls into a chair and Marie leaves the piano
and approaches without being heard.*)

MARIE.

But you must tell

Me all your sorrows. . .

ALBERT (*starting*).

Who is this ? 'tis you. . .

How came you here ? I thought you would not come

Again.

MARIE.

And why ?

ALBERT.

I scarcely know: I think
You do not like this studio. . .

MARIE.

I think
I have been to see you in a poorer place:
Have you forgotten quite Montmartre?

ALBERT.

Ah! no,
The little studio, underneath the slates.
You used to come and see me all the way,
Five flights of stairs.   How happy we were then!

MARIE.

Are you not happy here?

ALBERT.

Perhaps; but list:
I only know I love you, Marie,—all

My dreams, my thoughts, all sentiments of life
And death you gave me, and I have become
Only a part of you.

MARIE.

I know you love
Me ; you have been the sweetest and the best
Lover a woman ever kissed, and yet
The time will come when we shall meet as friends.

ALBERT.

But there have been lovers who did not part.

MARIE.

Perhaps, but such is not our lot, alas !
You know that we must say farewell for ever—
To-day.

ALBERT (*laughing*).

Of course, farewell ; we are indeed
No longer lovers.

MARIE.

Nay ; you must not jest.

ALBERT (*laughing*).

I must not jest, Marie ?   I never dreamt
Of jesting !

MARIE.

Have a little pity ; yea,
I know the truth.

ALBERT (*anxiously*).

What truth ?

MARIE.

Your marriage !

ALBERT.

Who

Has told you this ? I swear that it is false :
I never loved but you.—It is a lie !

MARIE.

I know the truth!

ALBERT (*hiding his face in his hands*).

I cannot marry her.

MARIE.

You must not weep, indeed—there is no use
In weeping : all have duties to perform,
And this is one of yours. . . .

ALBERT.

To say good-bye ?

MARIE.

Yea, even so!

ALBERT.

You want to rid yourself
Of me; I know you : this is some caprice,
A passionate whim of yours. And is he dark

Or fair ? and who is this Adonis ?—some
Dear friend of mine, for it is always so.

MARIE.

I have no other wish except to see
You happy, prosperous, and beloved by all
Who know you.

ALBERT.
I am happy here.

MARIE.

Do you remember in the ball-room, when
After the waltz we went to sit beneath
The laurels, how you leaned and suddenly
We kissed the first sweet kisses ?   All the night
I lay awake considering what were best
To do.   I reasoned well and strove against
Temptation, but my love was very strong,
For after many years of loveless life
'Tis harder to resist and firmly turn

Away from gladness, and refuse to touch
The lips that you have kissed a thousand times
In dream.   I knew that all must pass away
And sadly, but my heart said only this :
" Accept the last chance offered you—accept !
Your life is empty, you have only wealth,
And wealth is not enough."   I did accept,
And I have not regretted ; but I grow
Too old for you.   To-day your kisses are
A lover's, but in five years hence they will
Be nothing but a son's ; and you will spare
Me this humiliation.   Let us say
Good-bye.

ALBERT.

Nay, ask me not : alas ! I can
Do nothing, for my love is as a child's.
I would that we were lying fast asleep
Together in some quiet tomb afar
From all this trouble.   (*With passion.*)

Tell me, will you die
With me? and is not this occasion quite
Enchanting,—in this chamber hung with silk,
Encumbered everywhere with vases, flowers,
Venetian mirrors, Chinese ornaments,
And Turkish lamps?   On either side of this
Deep crimson sofa we will light and place
Two altar candles, and then lying down,
Not coiled together, but in one of those
Holy and simple poses that we often
See sculptured on the tombs in churches, breathe
Our souls away.

MARIE.

You dream of lovely dreams.
Alas! a modern lover never ends
So perfectly.   Your Blanche—you see I know
Her name—is very sweet, and you will learn
To love her better · · ·

ALBERT.

No, I gave what love
I had to give ; I have no more.

MARIE.

My dear,
I am to-day your mother, my desire
Is only that I may assist and help
You towards success and happiness in life,
And for this end we now must say good-bye.
But you shall come and see me when I have grown
A little older, with your wife ; and you
Shall bring your children with you,—I
Will love them for your sake, and they
Shall sit upon my knees.

ALBERT.

Alas ! let love
Burn slowly till it fades to ashes.

MARIE.

Nay,

I would preserve a perfect memory
Of love and happiness, and for this end
I bid you now farewell.

I bring you back

Your letters ; you have nothing now to fear.

(*She gives him a packet of letters, he looks at
them, and then she takes and throws them
into the fire.*)

And that you may be purified in fire

(*after a pause*)

I think that you had better give me mine.

(*He takes a packet of letters out of a drawer.*)

ALBERT.

I hoped to keep these letters for a link
To bind me to the past.

MARIE.

Old letters read
Distastefully.   I read some yesterday ;
They made me sad.

> (*She takes the packet and throws them into
> the fire.*)

ALBERT.

The flame devours each leaf
In turn, they grow from white to red and turn
To black ; we read a word, and then all fades
To senseless ashes, all is gone for aye,
And we are strangers with our faces set
On different stars, our feet on different roads ;
We do not know, it may have been a dream.

MARIE.

And life is even so.   One kiss : farewell !

> (*He kisses her.*)

ALBERT.

And shall I never see you any more?

MARIE.

After a year or two of marriage you
Must come and introduce me to your wife
And baby; all will be forgotten then,
And I will stand as godmother.   Farewell.

[*Exit.*   ALBERT *stands looking after her.*

BERNICE.

—

PALE in moonlight glistening
　Water-lilies lie,
I at window listening
Hear the fountain warble
Softly to the marble
　Breathing to the sky
　Echoes of a cry.

Upon the purple bosom of the night
The moon is dreaming softly, she doth seem
Like a pale beauty languidly reclining
Amid rich silken-cushioned canopies.
The winds are hushed, no breeze disturbs the scene,
Only the warbling of the fountain's song

And the full molten murmur of a bird
The silver silence break with melody.
The sultry air is filled with rose perfume
And soft-shed scent, whose wings upbear my soul
Higher than wildest music ever flew,
Into a heaven where mystic chords unite
Shadow with heat, the day unto the night.
Here in this garden, thro' the odorous summer,
I dream and satisfy my love with dreams
Of pleasure : one is stealing o'er me now,
And all my being shudders with delight.

   .   .   .   .

The flowers are moving, and I see a snake,
A monstrous many-coloured serpent : all
Her lingering length is trailing slowly down
A flight of marble stairs ; her eyes absorb
My soul as sunlight drinks the morning dew.
She slips along my naked side, between
My knees, along my body quite around

Leaning her close caressing head against
My face ; and sudden pains and pleasure pangs
Of brutalizing joy are crushing me
Amid the weight of her voluptuous coils.
But slowly they relax, and I arise
And feebly watch the moon : she sleeps—she sleeps.
Here in the shadow of the purple roses
I listen to the fountain murmuring
Softly, oh, softly, to the water-lilies,
The secret of Bernice.   I see her face
Arise from out the blanching water-flowers,
Her face of white rose, gazing on me sadly.
Oh, would I might forget ! but when I hearken
Unto this fountain's mazy murmuring
I fain would hear her story,—none is listening,—
The old sad tale of Bernice and the lilies.
No one is listening, all is silent here,
Yea, I can tell it softly, breathe it low,
In under-voice to this sweet purple rose.

    One summer night,—ah ! years have passed since then—

I sat with her beneath the oriel window,

Drinking the dreamy splendour of the moon

And the delirious perfumes of the night,

Till in my feverish flesh the blood took fire,

And love fell sick with famine for her face.

I held her feet between my hands, and laid

My head between her knees, and gazed upon

Her downward-gazing eyes in ecstacy.

I wound the heavy tresses of her hair

Across my face, and tried to weep: passion

Had dried my tears—life longèd unto death.

The demon of her destiny then spoke:

"The night is fair, let us stray down the garden

And sit beside the fountain where the lilies

Lie gazing on the moon.   It will be sweet

To bathe by night."   With linkèd hands we went

Unto the tiny lake of fountain born,

And bathed unwatched, alone, amid the flowers.

She was a vision of voluptuousness,

And over the water streamed her wondrous hair

Like braids of gold : she standing bosom-deep
Leaning from out the silver gleaming wave,
The love of all my years came over me,
Her lips were fast upon my face, I gazed
Within the vaporous languors of her eyes,
Until love's burden grew intolerable.
I know not how it was, her kisses stung,
Her bird-like throat full-filled with fluttering voice
Leaned over me, and all her sultry hair
Fell round my face.   The perfume of the roses
Drove me mad.   I know not how it was,
In kissing her I held her face beneath
The pallid water-flowers until it grew
More wan than they.   The roses were asleep,
The moon saw not between the darkling trees,
Only the lilies saw her drownèd face.
And now, through all the odorous summer nights,
I hearken to the fountain's warbling song,
Murmuring softly, oh, softly, to the lilies
The secret of Bernice, Love and Death.

Pale in moonlight glistening
  Water-lilies lie,
I at window listening
Hear the fountain warble,
Softly to the marble
  Breathing to the sky
  Echoes of a cry.

A JOYOUS DEATH.

LADIES of Love and mistresses, I have
Excluded all but you; around my bed
Weeping, you tell me of the good days dead,
You know that nothing new can help or save.

Watch the last watch, remember that you gave
Your promises that your hands should prepare
My body for the shroud, and that your fair
Shoulders should bear my coffin to the grave.

In later years I hope that you will meet
Often around my grave, and in the gathering gloom
Of evening tell how good I was and sweet.

And you shall be the gardeners of the place,
And pensively let each one come and trace
Her name for epitaph upon my tomb.

THE PORTRAIT.

—

PROLOGUE.

THE TRIUMPH OF THE FLESH.

WE have passed from the regions of dreams and of visions,
And the flesh is the flesh and the rose is the rose ;
And we see but the absolute joy of the present
     In the sunlight of beauty.

I am filled with carnivorous lust : like a tiger
I crouch and I feed on my beautiful prey :
There is nought in the monstrous world of Astarte
     So fair as thy body.

Let me lie, let me die on thy snow-coloured bosom,
I would eat of thy flesh as of delicate fruit,

I am drunk of its smell, and the scent of thy tresses
    Is as flame that devours.

Thou art demon and god, thou art hell, thou art heaven,
Thou art love that is lust, thou art lust that is love,
And I see but the heavenly grace of thy body,
    A picture—a poem,

    .   .   .   .

And the flesh is a soul, tho' it be not eternal.

SECOND PART.

THE TRIUMPH OF THE SOUL.

I LIVE alone, but I am never lonely
In these luxuriant chambers filled with flowers,
Italian vases, old engravings, pictures.

Surrounded with these relics of past ages,
That still retain the odour of your presence,
I live alone, but I am never lonely;

For you are here, and you will never leave me,
No more deceptions, weary idle grieving,
But peaceful ease and tender meditation.

So little and so much : a broad black velvet
Hat forming a circle round the face within it.—
At last my rooms have found a ministering spirit.

And you will watch me hour by hour for ever,
And never change the grand and strange expression
Of those brown eyes deep-set in crimson shadow.

I live alone, but I am never lonely;
For your eyes luminous with love and longing,
Like watching stars, burn softly through my dreaming.

Yea, even when I muse or write my poems,
I feel of instinct certain you are looking,
And then my soul grows happy and immortal.

And I am happy and my life is perfect,
Embalmed in dreams, the past lives on for ever—
The same old love, the same delightful passion.

All this will stay, there will be no more parting,
Nor sighs, nor tears, nor any bitter grieving,
But peaceful thoughts and tender meditation.

For, like a monk who weds his love ideal,
Beyond the busy hum of men and women,
I live alone, but I am never lonely.

And I am happy, for my love is perfect :
I drank with you the life of every passion ;
My memories are their disembodied spirits.

Life giveth much—I make no vain lamenting,
For verily I am deprived of nothing,
For was the past more perfect than the present ?

7

The past is past, but now I have the sweetness
Of looking back, and all my life is scented
With perfumed memories blown across the ocean

Across the seas around whose shores I wander,
Listening for ever to their wandering murmur:
The past and present are not twain, but single.

The ideal is the offspring of the real,
And in the child we have the mother's features,
Loving the one in memory of the other.

I live alone, but I am never lonely,
For you are here and you will never leave me,
And time can touch me not, nor any sorrow.

Delightful ease, perfumed with meditation,
Made holy by your sanctifying presence,
Shall fill my life with all its dreams of heaven!

For time can touch me not, nor any sorrow,
For you are here, and you will never leave me
Until the hour when all must part for ever. . .

Yet some assert that we may meet hereafter.

THIRD PART.

THE TRIUMPH OF TIME.

Now, after more than twenty years of living,
Of everything that constitutes existence,
I stand within these old deserted chambers.

The tapestries are full of dust and faded,
And spiders weave around the lofty windows;
And here were passed my early youth and manhood!

All things seem changed and altered: even the parrot
Is speaking new and unfamiliar phrases;
The old, alas! we both have well forgotten.

But nought is stirred; the flowers,—they have fallen
Across their painted urns in heavy tangles,
And spiders weave around the lofty windows.

Upon this sofa oft I lay composing
Sweet dreams of love and fancy into metre,
And now a verse I hardly can remember.

Upon this sofa oft I sat with women,
Kissing their raven tresses or their golden;
And where are they? and where are last year's roses?

Even their names are now well-nigh forgotten,
(The spiders weave around the lofty windows,)
And all the world is full of dreams and sorrows.

Ye poor old women, withered now and faded,
The years have spared but little—very sadly
Ye dream like me of goodly days gone over.

Perhaps the sweet love-hours we passed together
Are lingering places in your youthward wandering . . .
But where are you ? and where are last year's roses ?

And if we met, how sad a sight and useless !
Not one of you would know your former lover.
There is my portrait —'tis but little faded,

But by its side I see within the mirror
Reflected side by side another picture :
The half bald forehead of a man of fifty.

Yea, time with fierce hands drives us forward ever ;
Alas ! alas ! there is no sweet returning,
There is no rest until the final resting.

The books within the bookcase are forgotten,
And the authors dead . . . I read a dusty journal,
What once was news is now the oldest story.

And spiders'-webs hang round the lofty windows,
And in the drawers I find some faded letters ;
To read them seems almost an indiscretion.

Those words of love were written to another,
Unto the youth portrayed upon the canvas,
And not the man reflected in the mirror.

But turning now, I see another picture
Part hidden in a drapery half-fallen,—
Perhaps she was the writer of those letters . . .

It is the portrait of a lady :—shaded
Within the large hat forming quite a circle,
An oval face doth glisten like a jewel.

There is but little, one sweet tone of colour,
The dark eyes glow full-filled with southern languors,
The mouth burns crimson like a fiery blossom.

She holds a fan widespread across her bosom,
The pose is graceful : 'tis a sketch unfinished
And signèd by my dear friend Edward Manet.

Yes, yes, I now remember well the story :
He gave me that sweet pastel as a present,
Because he always said I was her lover.

It is the portrait of a Polish lady,—
I wonder if she is now dead or living,—
I loved her once, but love is soon forgotten.

Love is not soon forgot, but there is nothing
That time doth write not out with firm erasure ;
Sooner or later all must pass and perish.

The spiders weave around the lofty windows.

A NIGHT OF JUNE.

THE night was drowned
    And crowned
With over-much delight ;
    A breathless heat
    Too sweet
Made faint the sense and sight.

Hanging between
    The green
Of vine-inwoven bower,
    A plenilune
    In swoon
Glowed like a golden flower.

The shadows slept
    And crept

Like fairies to and fro,
    And roses hung
    And swung
Their censers high and low.

Her gleaming breast
    Was dressed
In clouds of amber hair ;
    And her breath came
    Like flame
Thro' the deep moon-lit air.

Her arms were wound
    Around
My downward gazing face ;
    And lips reposed
    And closed
Close kissing on the place.

Till passion's ache
    Could take

No new breath to respire;
   But sank to sleep
     In deep
Visions of blind desire.

Our souls were filled
    And stilled
With weight of heavenly tears,
   And sacred, glad
     And sad
Unreachable strange fears.

" Oh ! misery !
    Ah me ! "
She murmured o'er and o'er,
   " This night will pass,
     Alas !
As other nights before."

The moon doth bathe
    Her path

In liquid light and splendour ;
    As even so
    Doth glow
My soul with love most tender.

Life gives us gleams
    In dreams
Of something in swift flight,
    An instant star
    Afar
Lost in the deeps of night.

Joy and delight
    Are bright
Only a short-lived hour ;
    And day's too soon
    In June,
And love's too frail a flower.

IN THE MORNING.

LOOK yonder, swiftly shines the silver river,
The night has faded from the skies, the dawn
Is rising softly ; all the aspens shiver
In the cool keen breeze, the timid hind and fawn
   Are grazing on the lawn.

Our night of love is past, and over yonder
The sun-haze heaves, and there the wet-winged dove
Crosses from wood to wood. Come, let us wander
Out and assain our bodies of their love
   And all the fires thereof.

The night is done, and love is past and over,
This room perfumed of musk is hateful now.
Come, let us go, I am no more thy lover :

Are not my kisses colder far than snow
    And thine are even so.

Nay, thou art very weary of caresses
And their delight. Come, leave this flower-hung room
And deep divans and samite-hid recesses.
My brain is aching likewise of the fume
    Of smouldering perfume.

Nay, come, my sweet, and we will walk together
After the heat and turmoil of the night
Half friend-like and half lover-like, and gather
A few wild flowers in bunches red and white,
    All with the fresh dew bright.

And, as the wet leaves brush across our faces,
And chattering blackbirds fly across our way,
As we go wandering through the grass-grown places
Where a skylark pours forth his matin lay,
    Our thoughts shall pause and pray.

Yes, we shall pray, and our weak hearts be lifted
Unto the regions of pure thoughts and dreams,
Where all desires of sin and shame are sifted,
Till they may flow to Godward in sweet streams
      And glad effulgent beams.

The night is o'er, but it has not been wasted,
For though I kiss thee not, I love thee still,
Not as fierce wine is this time to be tasted,
But as the water of a shivering rill,
      Whose spring is sweet but chill.

The night is done, the bright bleak morning teaches
Us many things, sweet : let us go to-day,
Since it is day, and sit beneath the beeches,
Half friend-like and half lover-like, and say
      Why love outlasts not May.

THE TEMPLE OF TIME.

WEARY of sorrows and weary of pains, griefs,
     passions, and false joys,

Sadly I wandered in dream down to a desolate
     plain.

Faintly and bitter the moon shone over the
     mountainous headlands,

Over a grey-coloured sky filled with the wind
     of the night ;

Sound there was none but the sound of a storm-
     struck ocean lamenting,

Dark clouds wandered and cast shadows and
     torturous gleams.

Sadly I listened,—the ocean and sky said nothing
     but one word ;

Rock, stars, clouds, waves, moon echoed the
    ominous fate :

" Now or to-morrow, what matter if death be the
    certain and sure end ? "

Mine heart answered and said : " Nothing is
    sweeter than Death."

Held as a gained prey fast in the hard-struck
    talons of fell dreams,

Gazing I saw half-lost, hid in the glooms of the
    mist,

Walls of a temple gigantic, enclasped and
    resplendent with high gates,

Thrown back wide on the walls—portals as large
    as the world,

Where man enters to weep for awhile, there
    earning his rest time.

Forests of columns arose stately and grand in
    the gloom,

Which hung thickly and shrouded in tenebrous
    shadows the high roofs ;

Arch upon arch hung wide crossing in tangles
  like clouds

Over the mystic remote strange chapels en-
  tombed in a dark night

Where great silence was heard, infinite, vast and
  eternal.

Calm with the passion of dreaming, I sate down
  under a pillar,

Deep in the shadow, and there sadly I watched
  and I saw

Straying processions of dusk-draped figures re-
  passing before me;

Some were robed in white, others in blood-
  coloured robes.

Ever the other avoiding, they wandered in circles
  and knelt down,

Filled with the languors of hope, pale with the
  strength of despair,

Sadly in turn at the altars of Jove, Christ, Hela,
  Astarte,

8

Where all wearily sank sooner or later to Death,

Down in the ocean, beyond shoals, reefs, and
the foam of the shore surf.

New ones thronging refilled quickly the break
in the ranks

Scattered, and onward they went e'er seeking
the shadows that lured them,

Shaken of vision my soul cried in its bitterness out,

Lifting its eyes to the vast and titanic statue of
Tempus,

Who smiled cruelly down, filled with the splen-
dour of scorn :

" Say, great God, where leadest thou these thy
perishing soul-flocks ?

Which is the goal to be sought ? which is the
end that is best ?

Myriads of echoes replied all, giving an answer
the selfsame ;

Laughing and weeping in turn, mocking my
question, they said :

"Those are Desires,—look, headlong all soon
   drop by the wayside,

Vain hopes, false joys, griefs, sadly they carry
   to gods.—

God there is none save one God, Time is the
   infinite Godhead !

Bow down all, for the great guerdon he gives
   ye—is Death ! "

𝔖𝔬𝔫𝔫𝔢𝔱.

—

IDLY she yawned, and threw her heavy hair
Across her flesh-filled shoulders, called the maid,
And slipped her sweet blond body out of bed,
Searching her slippers in the wintry air.

The fire shed over all a sullen glare,—
Then in her bath she sponged from foot to head,
Her body, arms, breasts, thighs, and things unsaid,
Powdered and dried herself with delicate care.

Then Zoë entered with the *Figaro*,
The chocolate, the letters, and the cat,
And drew the blinds to show the falling snow.

Upon the sofa still her mistress sat
Drawing along her legs, as white as milk,
Her long stockings of finely-knitted silk.

BALLAD OF A LOVER OF LIFE.

MY days for loving and singing are over,
  For now I am stretched in the narrow bed
That the flowers and leaves and the wild grasses cover,
  And likewise the snow when the summer is dead.
  The bosoms where oft I have lain my head,—
Zara, and Lily, and Annie, and May,—
Like me are asleep in the common clay.
  But to ye who are giving or selling love's wares
To them who are feeble and foolish, I say
  My love was stronger and fiercer than theirs.

Ye golden moths that now flit and hover
  From the blossom of white to the blossom of red,
Remember me, for a lordly lover
  I was till the time allotted had sped,
  I would not be wholly forgotten, tho' fled

For aye from the place of your pleasure and play ;
Give a thought when unloosing your evening array,
In my years had you lived, my sighs and my prayers
Might have won you from weakly lovers away—
My love was stronger and fiercer than theirs.

I have passed into earth, no worm can discover
Much food in this body—to dust it is shed ;
I hear not the pipe of the wandering plover,
I hear not the sound of a passing tread ;
And yet the namesakes of women I wed
For the space of a year, a month, or a day,
Make merry with gallants as all maids may.
Could I wake I'd prove them the poorest of players ;
Had you known me you'd turn from them in dismay—
My love was stronger and fiercer than theirs.

ENVOI.

Prince was I ever of festival gay,
And time never silvered my locks with grey;

The love of your lovers is as hope that despairs,
  So think of me sometimes, dear ladies, I pray—
My love was stronger and fiercer than theirs.

AMBITION.

YEA, I would change my lot with any one,
A king, a scavenger, a courtezan,
A priest, a murderer, an artizan,
For nothing worth the doing have I done.

Just once, before I sleep beneath the stone,
I want to act and not to dream, I can ;
And leave within the future world of man
Some seed to blossom when I shall be gone.

If I am bad or good I little heed,
For are not all things vile or virtuous
According to the standard of our need ?

A soldier burnt the temple of Ephesus,—
It was, perhaps, a very dreadful deed,—
But it preserved his name, Erostratus.

A PAGE OF BOCCACE.

A CRIMSON light, all faint with delight,
   Steals thro' my lady's room,
And the scented air is moved by the rare
   Songs spun in the mystic loom
Of canaries' throats, whose untaught notes
   Float thro' the glimmer and gloom.

Dreaming she lies with fast-closed eyes
   Within the dim alcove,
As I bend over her she seems to stir
   With the instinct of my love,
For down the streams of her drifting dreams
   I may be the spirit above.

The breath from her mouth is like air from the south,
   It kisses my face and eyes,

And the touch of her hair which falls everywhere
   In restless harmonies,
My spirit doth wake to joys that break
   In a broken song of sighs.

She is bathed in the deep dream-mist of sleep
   Guided by love's faint ray,
In her lap's soft bed lies a book half read,
   A book I read yesterday;
It tells how human is soft sweet woman,
   How her love doth pass away.

     .   .   .   .

I gently took from her lap the book
   And opened it at the place,
That she waking might see how erringly
   A woman may run in love's race;
I awoke not her, but without a stir
   I dreamingly kissed her face.

Sonnet.

—

UNE FANTAISIE PARISIENNE.

YOU whispered quickly, and your words were warm
With dreams, and down the glistening marble flight
Of steps you passed me saying, "Come to-night,
The music told me of a tempting charm."

I saw you turn, I saw your gorgeous arm
Amid the silk and lace ; the electric light
Shed over all a mystical delight,
And vision filled my soul with sweet alarm,

Now wondering what your fancy might invent,
I pass a thickly carpeted saloon
To youward guided by the certain scent ;

Lifting a curtain suddenly,—what meets

My gaze ?—you, glittering like a precious stone

Amid the splendours of black satin sheets.

THE TEMPTATION.

SITTING in the silence, in the glimmer
Of my window where the light was dimmer,
    Gazing in the night,

Woman fairer than all mortal dreaming,
Weirdly lovely more than earthly seeming,
    Saw I in delight.

Wrapped in clouds of golden glittering tresses,
Stepped she swiftly from the dark recesses
    In the silver glare,

Stood beneath the moon, a white robe twining
Round her, hiding not the bosom shining
    Thro' her woven hair.

Like a lily seemed she, and a flower
Such as pallid passion doth devour
    Bore she in her hand.

That strange bloomless blossom born of vision,
Offering of a tired Love's derision,
    Held she to me, and

Kneeling at my feet, her white arms over
My face down drawn, speaking like a lover
    Words in symbols clothed,

Wooing in low quivering serpent hisses,
Crouching by me, feeding with live kisses
    Me, that longed yet loathed.

Then she, gathering me to burning bosom,
Gave to tempted lips the grievous blossom,
    Saying: "Taste of this . . .

" Nothing but a rose in shape and colour,
Sighing only tender light shed odour,
  Taste it in a kiss ! " . . .

Then I, overcome with weak'ning passion,
Mad'ning dreamings knowing no compassion,
  Drank the perfume deep.

But the breathings of the flower exotic
Stilled my senses like a soft narcotic
  Into mystic sleep,

Where the bridal bed was incense laden,
And with strangest flowers o'ershaden
  Shedding mystic calm,

And the overpowering airs were foison
With the languors of a subtle poison
  Soothing as a balm,

9

Where the bridegroom was a snake enfolden
Round me in a circle green and golden, . . .
    Whose undreamt desire

Did reveal me perilous joys ecstatic,
Troubled, visioned, sweetness enigmatic,
    Love reborn of fire . . .

Where the low and throbbing pleasures sicken,
And refluctuant sudden spasms quicken,
    Wearing out the soul,

Changing them to sterile, stagnant hour,
Where the trembling senses aching cower,
    Passed beyond the goal.

Such a sullen feverish dream I lay in
Till the morning chilly came by greying
    All the midnight skies.

Then I rose with many a shuddering shiver,
Tortured by the love that still did quiver
    In my waking sighs,

Vainly seeking, looking backward, even
Like an angel fallen from high heaven,
    Questioning every pain,

Sought I by some guessing known to no man
To unite the serpent and the woman
    In one vision twain.

Both had fled for ever, both were dreamings,
Phantoms seen in gleamings, mystic seemings,
    Things that never were.

Yet, there was beneath my bosom smitten,
Such small wound as serpent might have bitten
    Bleeding softly there.

THE HERMAPHRODITE.

"MARBLE most beautiful thou—
Thou art the dream that I dream :
Why standest thou pitiless there,
In the shade of the long green leaves ?
Why cannot my passion awaken,
Life in thy bosom of stone,
And give thee to love and me ? "
Said a young man weary and pale
(As a star when the morning is nigh)
Of febrile delight and desire.
Laying his face in his hands
He wept, and the silence was deep,
And the fountain murmured alone
To the beautiful blossoms and birds,
And a green light came from without

To mix with the crimson within,
And played o'er the purfled seats
Of a boudoir curtained with silk.

Arising, and weeping, he went
To the feet of a marble statue
That stood in a middle place,
A guardian goddess or god,
And softly his footsteps fell
Over the carpeted floor.
Then leaning he kissed the cold
White bosom—too bitterly cold—
And said, " O epicene maid,
In the dark dim sleep of creation
Wert thou unable as I
To choose, and turning too late
From the sensuous form of a girl
To the grander grace of a boy,
Attained but the height where love
And beauty untouched by the soiling

Stain of a sex remains,
A perfect immutable thing,
As useless to man as to God,
Belonging to neither—a dream
Belonging to poets alone."

Then the young man sank on the deep
Divan, and resting his head on his hand,
On his milk-white fingers, he gazed
Long on the statue.   It leaned
In a soft voluptuous pose
Like that of a leaning snake ;
And the face bent backward threw
Over the arms the tresses
Adown its feminine back,
And the boyish bosom was raised
By the movement upward, and on
It fell the principal light.

" I have lived on thy love in a world

Apart from the world of man,"
He said, as he raised his eyes
To watch the loll of the lovely
Limbs as they leaned in repose.
" Alas ! I have lived in a dream
Listening to febrile desires,
Chaunting the mystic acute
Strains of a song that explains
Nothing of human delight,
Strains that are tuneless and strange
To the common desire of man.
For even as thou art I am—
A strayed thing, straying beyond
The limits of actual love,
Into the kingdom of dream,
Where fruit there is none to gather—
Only the flower of a dream.

" But thou, what love would thy love
Seek in this world of ours ?

Would it be a girl's soft bosom,
Or the broad fair breast of a boy?
Or dost thou dream of the fond
Undreamable love of one
As fair and as strange as thyself?
Perfect indeed is the thought
Of what such a love might be,—
To die and to know not of God,
To love and to know not of hate,
To live and to know not of death,
Contented with life to joy
In the love of another as fair;
And to live for a while in the sight
Of infinite beauty as angels
Live in the presence of God.

I have loved only thee, and none other,
And known but the shadows of thee,
The dim blurred beauty that seemed
Sometimes like pictures of thee,

Pictures reflecting thy face.
But mortals are only motes
Seen in the passing rays,
And dreaming will never save,
Though immortal his dreams may be,
The dreamer the fate of the grave ;
For sooner or later we leave
The sunlight, the moonlight and flowers,
To sleep in the wet cold clay.
This is hard, but harder it is
To die without kissing but once
The face that we see in our dreams;
'Tis bitter to leave the world
Without attaining the end,
Leaving behind what you seek,
For if it exists in a dream
It must exist in the flesh."

He hid here his face in his hands
And wept, and the silence was deep,

And the fountain murmured alone
In the green conservatory, full
Of blossoms and birds, till at last
The silence was stirred by the voice
Of a page, who shouted in vain
To two great staghounds, that came
And bounded and gambolled in joy
Around their master who wept.

A MODERN POEM.

A SEA of green, a glittering sea of grass,
Before you, on the right and left, adorned
By groves of stately beeches, oaks,
And lofty elms and silent larches.   Far
The branches waved, their thousand shades of green
A violent, a delicate, a grey.
The distance on the right was planted thick
With pines: they grew amid the barren cliffs
Where a cascade fell sparkling in the sun.
Through the interspaces herds of browsing deer
Were wandering, sharply on the velvet turf
Their lengthening shadows were defined ; and some
Were stooping to the placid river's flow
To drink.   The stream was full of floating swans
And lilies ; here 'twas open to the sky,

And there amid the overhanging woods
'Twas lost a moment ; then it reappeared,
A-creeping through the meadows like a snake
Gliding away.   A rabbit started out
The sun-lit ferns, and scurried quickly towards
A neighbouring covert ; but the gamekeeper,
A hard-faced man attired in corduroy
And gaiters, lifted his gun and bowled him over.
A baldcoot fluttered through the reeds ; the deer
Bounded across the pastures of the park,
Across the hillocks through the elms and oaks,
Till lost within the brushwood on the left.
The keeper picked the kicking rabbit up,
And with a sharp stroke of his side-turned hand
He broke its back ; and, as he stuffed it in
The game-bag hanging o'er his shoulder, muttered,
" A couple o' brace of partridge and a brace
Of rabbits is enough," and forthwith turned
To leave them at the Manor.   Red and huge
It stood, approached by steps with balustrades

Where Irish setters slumbered in the sun,
And peafowl strutted haughtily. One wing
Was filled with Tudor windows, but the left
Was better Gothic. Poor Sir Hubert knew
Pugin, he cultivated taste and learned
A learned name which sounded strange amid
The senseless verbiage that he mumbled. Poor
Sir Hubert thought himself a perfect judge
Of pictures, but he could not tell, I think,
A Rubens from a Raphael. Many a man
Sows here instead of there, and wastes what might
Have been a useful life. Supposing he
Had loved his horses more and pictures less,
The good man would have left an honest name,
As did his ancestors, for riding hard
And bringing down the pheasant rocketing ;
And after dinner, when the wine goes round,
And memory awakes, each drinker would
Recall some anecdote and speak of him
As coming of the good old stock, instead

Of mumbling lame excuses : " Poor
Sir Hubert, he was very fond of art."
Sir George, the present baronet, is all
He should be : an honest country gentleman,
With no new-fangled notions.

                              Just enough
Of scholarship to talk in common ways
Of common things. He learned that Cæsar wrote
Good Latin, and he knew a dozen names
In ancient history, four in modern,—this
Was quite enough. And then he came to Kent,
To ride and shoot and marry. Wooing well,
He won his cousin Lucy, and he placed
The heir Sir George upon his father's knee.
Blessing his son, the old man died soon after,
Apparently contented with the way
That life had come to him ; perhaps there was
A weak regretting rambling in his breast,
Of some façades and windows, Gothic ones,
He had not added to the eastern wing ;

And perhaps that he had never seriously
Gone in for painting.

               George, his son, has lived
A life of broad contentment, and the years
Pass over seeing but very little change.
The death of Margaret, a girl as fair
And delicate as a cloud in summer, told
Him what there was of sorrow in the world
For him to bear.

              A massive cut-stone bridge
Led to the pleasure grounds. The laurels stretched
This side and that side, and the green alleys
Were rippling over with the crimson foam
Of many roses ; the flower-beds and vases
Were kept in perfect order, and the grass
Was closely shaven like a face. Within
A sheltered corner out o' the wind was laid
The tennis ground ; the courts were freshly marked
And rolled. A goodly company was there,—
A dozen county families at least.

Beneath the laurels and the flowering trees,
That cast a broad sweet shade across the sward,
The matrons and the players who awaited
Their turn to play were sitting, and they talked,
Watching the game, from time to time applauding
A stroke.   A foreigner would be surprised
To see these slender-waisted maidens run
And show such skill.   Miss Fanshaw was
A thin wee girl attired in bluish silk,
And as the coming champion all did speak
Of her.   Those English girls, so fair and fresh
With exercise and health, seemed strange to one
Accustomed to the cultivated dolls
Of Paris.   Quaint their aprons, 'broidered round
The edges with an olive green design,
And their dear jerseys innocently slim.
Miss Fanshaw then was playing in a double,
And with a switching cut she served the ball.
Well served, and well returned !   Jim Wright,
The county's champion player, ran and got

It up.   "Oh, played indeed!" the company cried,
Clapping their hands ; again it was sent back,
Again and once again, this time lobbed over,
Then with a cutting stroke returned until
Miss Fanshaw ran and killed it at the net,
Winning the game. Two powdered footmen wheeled
A table spread with teacups and decanters
Beneath the laurels ; Lady Marian filled
The cups, and Ellen, her daughter, strove to make
Another double.   "Lord Mount Henry, you
Had better play with Miss Fitzwilliam, Sir John
And Lady Florence."

               "What, Sir John! do you
Play tennis?" asked astonished Mrs. Ash,
A fresh and portly lady.   Her white hands
Were the sweet fruit of many centuries'
Idleness.

      "And pray why not?" he answered,
Laughing ; "my girls have taught it me. At first
They had to drag me out, but now I go

More willingly than they.   I thought indeed
My days for games were over, but it keeps
Me down in weight and up in spirits.

                                        "Tom
Will teach you," said he, quizzing her, and with
A nod he pointed out a stalwart lad,
Her son.   A real English boy, his fresh
Neck showed beneath his open tennis shirt;.
The light and graceful figure summoned up
The thought the Athenian sculptor felt when he
Beheld in some Greek youth the Disque-player.
A double and a single set being now arranged,
The latter for the county's championship,
A match looked forward to, Miss Summerville
Was free of duty.   She walked dreaming through
The laurels, through the pleasure grounds in all
Their summer pride of ornamental beds,
Flaring with flowers, and as she strolled along
The gravel walk, shading the tender pink
And whiteness of her face, too liable

To freckle, with a long-fringed parasol,

She looked most wonderfully modern ; the dark

Blue jersey showed her figure tall and slim

In all its gradual developments.

Taking the walk that led along the stream,

She wandered towards a spot she knew of.   Beeches

Extended huge majestic branches o'er

The river, there the ferns grew high, and there

The flowering rhododendrons filled the air

With colour, and the screening leaves were sprinkled

With the azure of the sky.   Beside the brink

She sat upon a fallen tree whose boughs

Lay in the flow ; contemplative and still,

She watched the water rippling through the lilies,

Which floated on the flow, regretfully

She dreamt, recalling pleasant hours and days,

And ghost-like she returned upon the past,

Gliding adown its current, pausing here

And there at dated days.   Her life had been

A summer-coloured picture filled with scenes

Of animal enjoyments.   There were balls
Where silver-shouldered women rustling glode
Through parquèd drawing-rooms magnificent
With light; the moving mass of colour stained
With blackcoats peeping through; and oh, the wit
And laughter!   Supper tables covered o'er
With jellies, creams, and lobster salads, wings
Of chicken eaten, glasses of champagne
Drunken between the rapturous waltzes ; then
The moments when she sat in the rotund
Amid the long cool plants, and talked in whispers,
In hearing of the music.   Softly her dream
Wandered, and Ellen on a chestnut nag
Is standing near some furze and larches. "Hark!
To admiral," cries the huntsman, and the pack
Run rushing to the spot and verify
A find!   "Take care, you'll head him," cries the whip,
As he comes galloping along.   "No fear
Of that : look there, this side he's broke," they cry,
And Reynard streams away across the fields,—

Sun-lit delicious pasture-lands, whose green
Is speckled here and there with tillage. Through
The boundary fence the hounds are pouring, now
They settle to the scent and drive along
In all the silent ecstacy of pace.
"Forward!" cries one and "Line" another, as
They cram their horses at a double rail.
The chestnut flies it; "Jove! how well she rides!"
Cries many a stopping man. The hounds in view
Cross furrow and ridge with lowered sterns and bristles
Erect; a hedge succeeds a rail, a ditch
A gate; and on we go, at every fence
Diminishing in number. Sweet the air;
The sky is dappled o'er with sun-lit clouds,
The dew is on the grass. At last, thank God,
A check. The panting horses get their wind;
But few are there,—the chestnut is. They try
A cast, the hounds disperse a moment; then
Away they go across the grassy plains,
Broken by woods and dotted here and there

By standard trees.   The hounds are hunting now;
Along the hedgerows how they turn, they wheel
Like pigeons, following every trace of scent.
He steals along this fencing, black with mire,
His narrow, knavish-looking countenance
Intent on his pursuers, running for
His life.   The hounds are through; he turns and shows
His teeth.   They tumble over him in fierce
And hungry confusion.   Crash! and comes
A horseman through the rail, and through the gap
Another; higher up the chestnut rises,
And safely lands this side.

                She got the brush
And many compliments; 'tis hanging up
Over the fireplace in her room.

                   Her dream
Wanders to other scenes: she sees herself
Feeding her pigeons in the poultry-yard,
And ordering dinner as they fly around
Her head.   The cook is obstinate, the bills

Are high, and everything is running wrong
Through vexing ways and channels.   In the post
There is much consolation ; here it comes !
No letters ! but a fresh relay of books,
And Ouida's latest !—pleasant it will be,
When all the household work is done to sit
From twelve to two perusing lazily
The novel in a rocking-chair, a-hid
Beneath the trees upon the lawn, and grow
Quite sentimental in the sunlight.   Jack
And Willy love her well, as well as men
Have ever loved, and she loves Jack the best
Of all.   It matters little now : the past
Is dead for aye, although its features yet
Are warm, for she will wed Lord Haughington.
He was indifferent to her,—a tall
Spare man, with wide shoulders and a thin
Neck, and a somewhat vacant stare in his
Chilly blue eyes, a ceremonious way
Of talking to you : this was right and that

Was wrong, and such things could not be.

The birds

Flew in and out amid the scrubby bushes
That grew along the water's edge ; they pecked,
Flirted and quarrelled 'mid the rustling leaves.
The sensual silent softness of the place
Was dear to sadness, and adown the tides
The swans came floating, basking in the sun ;
The sweet persuasive perfumes of the earth,
The woods, the plants and flowers, floated and filled
The golden light, and all around was heard
The musical emotion of the world.

As sailors watch from their prison
    For the long grey line of the coasts,
I look to the past rearisen,
    And joys come over in hosts
    Like the white sea-birds from their roosts.

I love not th' indelicate present,
    The future's unknown to our quest,

To-day is the life of the peasant,
But the past is a haven of rest,—
The joy of the past is the best.

The rose of the past is better
Than the rose we ravish to-day ;
'Tis holier, purer, and fitter
To place on the shrine where we pray,—
For the secret thoughts we obey.

There, are no deceptions nor changes,
There, all is placid and still ;
No grief, nor fate that estranges,
Nor hope that no life can fulfil ;
But ethereal shelter from ill.

The coarser delights of the hour
Tempt, and debauch and deprave ;
And we joy in a poisonous flower,
Knowing that nothing can save
Our flesh from the fate of the grave.

But surely we leave them, returning
   In grief to the well-loved nest,
Filled with an infinite yearning,
   Knowing the past to be rest—
   That the things of the past are the best.

Ellen re-lived her girlhood in the dreams
That came and flitted like the birds ; she sat
And wondered what the future had in store
For her.   The flaxen hair just tinged with gold
Was slipping o'er her shoulders, vacantly
Her blue eyes watched the birds, sweet eyes
That told the delicate story of her chaste
And healthy life.   Her face, a little long,
Was very pale—her mouth, a flower of blood,
Was large—her throat was white and flexible,
Her figure slim and graceful, like a deer's.
Though Ellen loved the excitement of the hounds
And tennis lawn, her heart was filled with love
Even as a flower with odour.   She had dreamed

Delicious girlish dreams as delicate

As gossamer, and purer than its dew ;

Yet not the febrile stuff ascribed to girls,

But wholesome passion born of wholesome flesh.

Who is the lover of the modern maid ?

We all have seen him and admired his tall

Figure and fearless English face, and Ellen

Had heard his manly love proposed, had felt

The warm caressing pressure of his hand ;--

But all is nothing, everything is nought,

The banquet passes, and no bill of fare

Is needed,- -there's the solitary dish,

Eat and be satisfied.   And so her dreams

Rambled until the approaching sound of steps

Coming along the gravel called her thoughts

From reveries.   Surprised, she rose to meet

Lord Haughington ; grey hair replaced the black,

A cold bleak smile a joyful one, and thus

The real uncrowns the empire of the dream.

She gave her hand—he broke the silence first

With ordinary words. "I thought to meet
You on the tennis ground.   This is a place
To find ' Il Penseroso.'   Are not these
High-arching trees, so solemn and so calm,
Unsuited to ' L'Allegro's ' character ?"
"The twain are one ; the separation is
Merely poetic licence," she returned,
With rippling laughs and smiles. "But since you think
Me so prosaic, tell me why you came
To find me here.—I compliment myself
It was not me you came to seek."

                  "Not so ;
But still I thought you loved the poetry
Of pleasure more than that of sadness."

                      "Yes,
I think I do."

          "You asked me to betray,"
He answered, striving to be humourous,
"The confidence of kind informing friends ?
I will be frank : 'twas Lady Marian ;

She said that frequently you went to feed
Your swans at evening."

     " Yes, I merely thought
To throw the bits of bread I saved for them
At lunch, and then regain my company,"
She answered hurriedly ; " I think I must
Return to them."

     " I hope," he murmured gravely,
" I shall not be deprived of seeing you feed
Your swans and cygnets."

      " If you care to see
Them, come this way ; I think that we shall find
Them near the waterfall : I know their haunts."

Gaily, but with affected glee, she talked
Of common topics, knowing well that this
Was the occasion he desired—that he
Was following each expression ; any word
Or phrase might be the stepping stone desired
For. If she talked of flowers, he might at once

Tell her she was the fairest of them all,

Or if she spoke of fashions, he would gaze

And say she never looked so well.   She dared

Not linger,—every subject nervously

She skirted, just as if each phrase concealed

The dreaded precipice ; for well she knew

That if he asked her for her hand, although

The payment with her lips was sour, she had

Scarcely the moral courage to resist.

Against an azure arch of sky they went,

A vista leading to the open park ;—

Reaches of velvet turf extended, green

Beneath their feet, but greying as it stretched

Into the distance, till it touched the far

Horizon, where the sun had flooded all

With gold.   They strolled beneath the sombre cedars

Which grew this side o' the bridge, gigantic trees

Whose shade fell o'er the sun-lit meadow down

To the river.   Swans and cygnets, all the brood,

Were swimming in and out the arches.   From

The parapet she threw them bits of bread ;—
He watched her white hands whiter than the birds,
Lifted to throw.

         Did he admire her ?   Say
He loved her as an honourable wife,
And all is said.

         He could not love : the power
To love is learned, the sentiment acquired,
For every passion cultivates the heart
To bear a better and a richer fruit.
But those who have not love can buy : an hour,
A day, a year, a lifetime if you will.
Money does all things : it can pluck and place
That lovely lily in a golden vase
To die.   The price makes pure, for certainly
In gold, not water, is the modern world
Baptized.   A hushed, a tender calm was felt,
The sunlight fell in heavy drops upon
The water-lilies, but the solemn man
Who stood beside her leaning against the bridge

Felt little of his unloved youth arise
Within his veins.   The story of his life
At full length lies within a paragraph.
After his college days he made a tour
Through Europe : Paris he had seen, and Rome ;
He knew them as the starer in the crowd
The colour of a passing lady's dress.   He went
To see the world, as was befitting his
Position.   London drawing-rooms, the best,
Were open to him ; but he never gained
The triumphs of the salon.   Ladies tired
His graver mind with all their fanciful
Futilities,—he felt he wearied them ;

And in the club-room he was voted just
A well-bred bore.   His loves in Chelsea proved,
After repeated absolutions, still
Very unfaithful ; and a thousand dropped at cards
Convinced him that the quietude of Kent
Was better suited to his special mind.

And there his tenantry and his estate
Gave him sweet occupation—there he found
His mission—there he found that every life
May be resolved to good account.   And so
The solemn years passed by in soft and grey
Succession, till the thought of lonely age,
Childless and wifeless, came to haunt him ; first
It was a wandering thought, but soon it fixed
Itself for ever in his mind.

                The last
Morsel of bread being given, Ellen turned
To go ; but laying his hand upon her arm,
He said the simple words that every man
Must say : he asked her with much dignity,
Yet not without a touch of tenderness,
To be his wife.   She raised her faint blue eyes
And murmured low, without embarrassment—
"I will, Lord Haughington." This grave grey man
Had never played the lover, and the joys
Of sensuous vows and kisses could be guessed

But dimly, yet he felt that he had missed
An inner portion of this life of ours.
He could not think that a Lord Haughington
Usurped another's place, but yet he felt
He was antithetical to this sweet girl
Feeding her swans at eventide.   The sun
Sank slowly over the horizon, drowned
Little by little in a bath of gold.
The river glittered in the lingering light,
Reflecting all the stillness of the reeds
And trees.   They turned to-homewards silently,
Plucking the leaves and roses as they went
Through the dark laurels and the flowering trees
That filled the woods adjacent to the house.
The evening air tasted of flowers and fruit,
And from afar they heard the pearly laughs
Of many nightingales.   They passed along
The emptying tennis lawn, where still some three
Or four were playing, whilst the others stood
Upon the steps and strolled around the sweep.

Then Ellen and Lord Haughington rejoined
The company.   To stay to dinner some
Had been invited ; the others sought their wraps
And ordered round their carriages.   A group
Stood wishing Lady Marian good-bye.
She spoke but little, getting rid of them
With short and single phrases, while she watched
Her daughter nervously, and strove to read
'Accepted' in her eyes.   Her last friend gone,
And from the clucking talk of one young man,
Who lingered yet, escaping, she rejoined,
Her daughter.   Ellen murmured just a word
Anent the evening and the swans, and passed
To bid adieu to some departing guest,
Leaving her mother and Lord Haughington
Alone.   With expectation all were still,
Brothers and sisters, friends and company.
And as along the leafy avenues
The carriages and phætons rolled, all drew
Together, whispering that she was engaged.

Ellen stood on the steps and watched the stars,

The passionless pale planets that appeared

From time to time adown the blue expanse,

Lost and absorbed by the magnetic charm

Of space, till startled suddenly by steps.

A young man passed from out the hall ; he stopped

And held his hand to her ; she took it, saying,

"I could not help it : you will not forget

The pleasant times that we have had, the times . . .

Forgive me and forget me, dearest Jack."

04